Bandit Algorithms for Website Optimization

John Myles White

O'REILLY®

Beijing · Cambridge · Farnham · Köln · Sebastopol · Tokyo

Bandit Algorithms for Website Optimization

by John Myles White

Published by O'Reilly Media, Inc., 1005 Gravenstein Highway North, Sebastopol, CA 95472.

O'Reilly books may be purchased for educational, business, or sales promotional use. Online editions are also available for most titles (*http://my.safaribooksonline.com*). For more information, contact our corporate/institutional sales department: 800-998-9938 or *corporate@oreilly.com*.

Editors: Mike Loukides and Meghan Blanchette
Production Editor: Christopher Hearse

Proofreader: Christopher Hearse
Cover Designer: Randy Comer
Interior Designer: David Futato
Illustrator: Rebecca Demarest

December 2012:   First Edition

Revision History for the First Edition:

2012-12-07   First release

See *http://oreilly.com/catalog/errata.csp?isbn=9781449341336* for release details.

ISBN: 978-1-449-34133-6

LSI

Table of Contents

Preface

Finding the Code for This Book

This book is about algorithms. But it's not a book about the theory of algorithms. It's a short tutorial introduction to algorithms that's targetted at people who like to learn about new ideas by experimenting with them in practice.

Because we want you to experiment, this book is meant to be read while you're near an interpreter for your favorite programming language. In the text, we illustrate every algorithm we describe using Python. As part of the accompanying online materials, there is similar code available that implements all of the same algorithms in Julia (*http:// julialang.org*), a new programming language that is ideally suited for implementing bandit algorithms. Alongside the Python and Julia code, there are also links to similar implementations in other languages like JavaScript.

We've chosen to use Python for this book because it seems like a reasonable lingua franca for programmers. If Python isn't your style, you should be able to translate our Python code into your favorite programming language fairly easily.

Assuming you are happy using Python or Julia, you can find the code for the book on GitHub at *https://github.com/johnmyleswhite/BanditsBook*. If you find mistakes or would like to submit an implementation in another language, please make a pull request.

Dealing with Jargon: A Glossary

While this book isn't meant to introduce you to the theoretical study of the Multiarmed Bandit Problem or to prepare you to develop novel algorithms for solving the problem, we want you to leave this book with enough understanding of existing work to be able to follow the literature on the Multiarmed Bandit Problem. In order to do that, we have to introduce quite a large number of jargon words. These jargon words can be a little odd at a first, but they're universally used in the academic literature on Multiarmed Bandit Problems. As you read this book, you will want to return to the list of jargon words below to remind yourself what they mean. For now, you can glance through them, but we don't expect you to understand these words yet. Just know that this material is here for you to refer back to if you're ever confused about a term we use.

Reward

> A quantitative measure of success. In business, the ultimate rewards are profits, but we can often treat simpler metrics like click-through rates for ads or sign-up rates for new users as rewards. What matters is that (A) there is a clear quantitative scale and (B) it's better to have more reward than less reward.

Arm

> What options are available to us? What actions can we take? In this book, we'll refer to the options available to us as arms. The reasons for this naming convention will be easier to understand after we've discuss a little bit of the history of the Multiarmed Bandit Problem.

Bandit

> A bandit is a collection of arms. When you have many options available to you, we call that collection of options a Multiarmed Bandit. A Multiarmed Bandit is a mathematical model you can use to reason about how to make decisions when you have many actions you can take and imperfect information about the rewards you would receive after taking those actions. The algorithms presented in this book are ways of trying to solve the problem of deciding which arms to pull when. We refer to the problem of choosing arms to pull as the Multiarmed Bandit Problem.

Play/Trial

> When you deal with a bandit, it's assumed that you get to pull on each arm multiple times. Each chance you have to pull on an arm will be called a play or, more often, a trial. The term "play" helps to invoke the notion of gambling that inspires the term "arm", but the term trial is quite commonly used.

Horizon

> How many trials will you have before the game is finished? The number of trials left is called the horizon. If the horizon is short, you will often use a different strategy than you would use if the horizon were long, because having many chances to play each arm means that you can take greater risks while still having time to recover if anything goes wrong.

Exploitation

> An algorithm for solving the Multiarmed Bandit Problem *exploits* if it plays the arm with the highest estimated value based on previous plays.

Exploration

An algorithm for solving the Multiarmed Bandit Problem *explores* if it plays any arm that does not have the highest estimated value based on previous plays. In other words, exploration occurs whenever exploitation does not.

Explore/Exploit Dilemma

The observation that any learning system must strike a compromise between its impulse to explore and its impulse to exploit. The dilemma has no exact solution, but the algorithms described in this book provide useful strategies for resolving the conflicting goals of exploration and exploitation.

Annealing

An algorithm for solving the Multiarmed Bandit Problem *anneals* if it explores less over time.

Temperature

A parameter that can be adjusted to increase the amount of exploration in the Softmax algorithm for solving the Multiarmed Bandit Problem. If you decrease the temperature parameter over time, this causes the algorithm to anneal.

Streaming Algorithms

An algorithm is a streaming algorithm if it can process data one piece at a time. This is the opposite of batch processing algorithms that need access to all of the data in order to do anything with it.

Online Learning

An algorithm is an online learning algorithm if it can not only process data one piece at a time, but can also provide provisional results of its analysis after each piece of data is seen.

Active Learning

An algorithm is an active learning algorithm if it can decide which pieces of data it wants to see next in order to learn most effectively. Most traditional machine learning algorithm are not active: they passively accept the data we feed them and do not tell us what data we should collect next.

Bernoulli

A Bernoulli system outputs a 1 with probability p and a 0 with probability $1 - p$.

Conventions Used in This Book

The following typographical conventions are used in this book:

Italic

Indicates new terms, URLs, email addresses, filenames, and file extensions.

Constant width

> Used for program listings, as well as within paragraphs to refer to program elements such as variable or function names, databases, data types, environment variables, statements, and keywords.

Constant width bold

> Shows commands or other text that should be typed literally by the user.

Constant width *italic*

> Shows text that should be replaced with user-supplied values or by values determined by context.

 This icon signifies a tip, suggestion, or general note.

 This icon indicates a warning or caution.

Using Code Examples

This book is here to help you get your job done. In general, if this book includes code examples, you may use the code in this book in your programs and documentation. You do not need to contact us for permission unless you're reproducing a significant portion of the code. For example, writing a program that uses several chunks of code from this book does not require permission. Selling or distributing a CD-ROM of examples from O'™Reilly books does require permission. Answering a question by citing this book and quoting example code does not require permission. Incorporating a significant amount of example code from this book into your product'™s documentation does require permission.

We appreciate, but do not require, attribution. An attribution usually includes the title, author, publisher, and ISBN. For example: "*Bandit Algorithms for Website Optimization* by John Myles White. Copyright 2013 John Myles White, 978-1-449-34133-6."

If you feel your use of code examples falls outside fair use or the permission given above, feel free to contact us at *permissions@oreilly.com*.

Safari® Books Online

 *Safari Books Online* is an on-demand digital library that delivers expert content in both book and video form from the world's leading authors in technology and business.

Technology professionals, software developers, web designers, and business and creative professionals use Safari Books Online as their primary resource for research, problem solving, learning, and certification training.

Safari Books Online offers a range of product mixes and pricing programs for organizations, government agencies, and individuals. Subscribers have access to thousands of books, training videos, and prepublication manuscripts in one fully searchable database from publishers like O'Reilly Media, Prentice Hall Professional, Addison-Wesley Professional, Microsoft Press, Sams, Que, Peachpit Press, Focal Press, Cisco Press, John Wiley & Sons, Syngress, Morgan Kaufmann, IBM Redbooks, Packt, Adobe Press, FT Press, Apress, Manning, New Riders, McGraw-Hill, Jones & Bartlett, Course Technology, and dozens more. For more information about Safari Books Online, please visit us online.

How to Contact Us

Please address comments and questions concerning this book to the publisher:

O'Reilly Media, Inc.
1005 Gravenstein Highway North
Sebastopol, CA 95472
800-998-9938 (in the United States or Canada)
707-829-0515 (international or local)
707-829-0104 (fax)

We have a web page for this book, where we list errata, examples, and any additional information. You can access this page at *http://oreil.ly/bandit-algorithms-optimization*.

To comment or ask technical questions about this book, send email to *bookquestions@oreilly.com*.

For more information about our books, courses, conferences, and news, see our website at *http://www.oreilly.com*.

Find us on Facebook: *http://facebook.com/oreilly*

Follow us on Twitter: *http://twitter.com/oreillymedia*

Watch us on YouTube: *http://www.youtube.com/oreillymedia*

Acknowledgments

This minibook has benefitted from years of discussions about the Explore-Exploit problem that I've had with the members of Princeton's psychology department. My thanks go to them, as well as to the three technical reviewers—Matt Gershoff at Conductrics, Roberto Medri at Esty, and Tim Hopper at RTI—all of whom read through this book and found countless ways to improve it. Their comments were invaluable and I'm deeply appreciative for all of the little errors that they kept from creeping into the final release of this book. Finally, I'd like to thank the various people who've contributed to the codebase on bandit algorithms that complements this book. Receiving pull requests contributing supplemental code for a book that wasn't even released has been among my favorite experiences ever as an author.

CHAPTER 1

Two Characters: Exploration and Exploitation

To set the stage for this book, I'm going to tell you a short story about a web developer, Deborah Knull, who ran a small web business that provided most of her income. Deb Knull's story will introduce the core concepts that come up when studying bandit algorithms, which are called *exploration* and *exploitation*. To make those ideas concrete, I'm going to associate them with two types of people: a scientist who explores and a businessman who exploits. My hope is that these two characters will help you understand why you need to find a way to balance the desires of both of these types of people in order to build a better website.

The Scientist and the Businessman

One Sunday morning, a young web enterpreneur, Deb Knull, came to suspect that changing the primary color of her site's logo would make her site's users feel more comfortable. Perhaps more importantly, she thought that making her customers feel more comfortable would make them buy more of the products her site was selling.

But Deb Knull worried that a new color could potentially disorient users and make them feel less comfortable. If that were true, her clever idea to increase sales might actually make her users buy fewer products instead. Unsure which of her instincts to trust, she asked for advice from two of her friends: Cynthia, a scientist, and Bob, a businessman.

Cynthia the Scientist

Cynthia, the scientist, loved Deb's proposed logo change. Excited by the opportunity to try out someting new, Cynthia started to lecture Deb about how to test her change carefully: "You can't just switch your logo to a new color and then assume that the change in the logo's color is responsible for whatever happens next. You'll need to run a controlled experiment. If you don't test your idea with a controlled experiment, you'll never know whether the color change actually helped or hurt your sales. After all, it's going to be Christmas season soon. If you change the logo now, I'm sure you'll see a huge increase in sales relative to the last two months. But that's not informative about the merits of the new logo: for all you know, the new color for your logo might actually be hurting sales."

"Christmas is such a lucrative time of year that you'll see increased profits despite having made a bad decision by switching to a new color logo. If you want to know what the real merit of your idea is, you need to make a proper apples-to-apples comparison. And the only way I know how to do that is to run a traditional randomized experiment: whenever a new visitor comes to your site, you should flip a coin. If it comes up heads, you'll put that new visitor into Group A and show them the old logo. If it comes up tails, you'll put the visitor into Group B and show them the new logo. Because the logo you show each user is selected completely randomly, any factors that might distort the comparison between the old logo and new logo should balance out over time. If you use a coinflip to decide which logo to show each user, the effect of the logo won't be distorted by the effects of other things like the Christmas season."

Deb agreed that she shouldn't just switch the color of her logo over; as Cynthia the scientist was suggesting, Deb saw that she needed to run a controlled experiment to assess the business value of changing her site's logo.

In Cynthia's proposed A/B testing setup, Groups A and B of users would see slightly different versions of the same website. After enough users had been exposed to both designs, comparisons between the two groups would allow Deb to decide whether the proposed change would help or hurt her site.

Once she was convinced of the merits of A/B testing, Deb started to contemplate much larger scale experiments: instead of running an A/B test, she started to consider comparing her old black logo with six other colors, including some fairly quirky colors like purple and chartreuse. She'd gone from A/B testing to A/B/C/D/E/F/G testing in a matter of minutes.

Running careful experiments about each of these ideas excited Cynthia as a scientist, but Deb worried that some of the colors that Cynthia had proposed testing seemed likely to be much worse than her current logo. Unsure what to do, Deb raised her concerns with Bob, who worked at a large multinational bank.

Bob the Businessman

Bob heard Deb's idea of testing out several new logo colors on her site and agreed that experimentation could be profitable. But Bob was also very skeptical about the value of trying out some of the quirkier of Cynthia's ideas.

"Cynthia's a scientist. Of course she thinks that you should run lots of experiments. She wants to have knowledge for knowledge's sake and never thinks about the costs of her experiments. But you're a businesswoman, Deb. You have a livelihood to make. You should try to maximize your site's profits. To keep your checkbook safe, you should only run experiments that could be profitable. Knowledge is only valuable for profit's sake in business. Unless you really believe a change has the potential to be valuable, don't try it at all. And if you don't have any new ideas that you have faith in, going with your traditional logo is the best strategy."

Bob's skepticism of the value of large-scale experimentation rekindled Deb's concerns earlier: the threat of losing customers was greater than Deb had felt when energized by Cynthia's passion for designing experiments. But Deb also wasn't clear how to decide which changes would be profitable without trying them out, which seemed to lead her back to Cynthia's original proposal and away from Bob's preference for tradition.

After spending some time weighing Cynthia and Bob's arguments, Deb decided that there was always going to be a fundamental trade-off between the goals that motivated Cynthia and Bob: a small business couldn't afford to behave like a scientist and spend money gaining knowledge for knowledge's sake, but it also couldn't afford to focus short-sightedly on current profits and to never try out any new ideas. As far as she could see, Deb felt that there was never going to be a simple way to balance the need to (1) learn new things and (2) profit from old things that she'd already learned.

Oscar the Operations Researcher

Luckily, Deb had one more friend she knew she could turn to for advice: Oscar, a professor who worked in the local Department of Operations Research. Deb knew that Oscar was an established expert in business decision-making, so she suspected the Oscar would have something intelligent to say about her newfound questions about balancing experimentation with profit-maximization.

And Oscar was indeed interested in Deb's idea:

"I entirely agree that you have to find a way to balance Cynthia's interest in experimentation and Bob's interest in profits. My colleagues and I call that the Explore-Exploit trade-off."

"Which is?"

"It's the way Operations Researchers talk about your need to balance experimentation with profit-maximization. We call experimentation *exploration* and we call profit-maximization *exploitation*. They're the fundamental values that any profit-seeking system, whether it's a person, a company or a robot, has to find a way to balance. If you do too much exploration, you lose money. And if you do too much exploitation, you stagnate and miss out on new opportunities."

"So how do I balance exploration and exploitation?"

"Unfortunately, I don't have a simple answer for you. Like you suspected, there is no universal solution to balancing your two goals: to learn which ideas are good or bad, you have to explore — at the risk of losing money and bringing in fewer profits. The right way to choose between exploring new ideas and exploiting the best of your old ideas depends on the details of your situation. What I can tell you is that your plan to run A/B testing, which both Cynthia and Bob seem to be taking for granted as the only possible way you could learn which color logo is best, is not always the best option."

"For example, a trial period of A/B testing followed by sticking strictly to the *best* design afterwards only makes sense if there is a definite best design that consistently works across the Christmas season and the rest of the year. But imagine that the best color scheme is black/orange near Halloween and red/green near Christmas. If you run an A/B experiment during only one of those two periods of time, you'll come to think there's a huge difference — and then your profits will suddenly come crashing down during the other time of year."

"And there are other potential problems as well with naive A/B testing: if you run an experiment that streches across both times of year, you'll see no average effect for your two color schemes — even though there's a huge effect in each of the seasons if you had examined them separately. You need context to design meaningful experiments. And you need to experiment intelligently. Thankfully, there are lots of algorithms you can use to help you design better experiments."

The Explore-Exploit Dilemma

Hopefully the short story I've just told you has made it clear to you that you have two completely different goals you need to address when you try to optimize a website: you need to (A) learn about new ideas (which we'll always call *exploring* from now on), while you also need to (B) take advantage of the best of your old ideas (which we'll always call *exploiting* from now on). Cynthia the scientist was meant to embody exploration: she was open to every new idea, including the terrible ideas of using a purple or chartreuse logo. Bob was meant to embody exploitation, because he closes his mind to new ideas prematurely and is overly willing to stick with tradition.

To help you build better websites, we'll do exactly what Oscar would have done to help Deborah: we'll give you a crash course in methods for solving the Explore-Exploit dilemma. We'll discuss two classic algorithms, one state-of-the-art algorithm and then refer you to standard textbooks with much more information about the huge field that's arisen around the Exploration-Exploitation trade-off.

But, before we start working with algorithms for solving the Exploration-Exploitation trade-off, we're going to focus on the differences between the bandit algorithms we'll present in this book and the tradition A/B testing methods that most web developers would use to explore new ideas.

CHAPTER 2

Why Use Multiarmed Bandit Algorithms?

What Are We Trying to Do?

In the previous chapter, we introduced the two core concepts of exploration and exploitation. In this chapter, we want to make those concepts more concrete by explaining how they would arise in the specific context of website optimization. When we talk about "optimizing a website", we're referring to a step-by-step process in which a web developer makes a series of changes to a website, each of which is meant to increase the success of that site. For many web developers, the most famous type of website optimization is called Search Engine Optimization (or SEO for short), a process that involves modifying a website to increase that site's rank in search engine results. We won't discuss SEO at all in this book, but the algorithms that we will describe can be easily applied as part of an SEO campaign in order to decide which SEO techniques work best.

Instead of focusing on SEO, or on any other sort of specific modification you could make to a website to increase its success, we'll be describing a series of algorithms that allow you to measure the real-world value of any modifications you might make to your site(s).

But, before we can describe those algorithms, we need to make sure that we all mean the same thing when we use the word "success." From now on, we are only going to use the word "success" to describe measurable achievements like:

Traffic
> Did a change increase the amount of traffic to a site's landing page?

Conversions
> Did a change increase the number of one-time vistors who were successfully converted into repeat customers?

Sales

Did a change increase the number of purchases being made on a site by either new or existing customers?

CTR's

Did a change increase the number of times that visitors clicked on an ad?

In addition to an unambiguous, quantitative measurement of success, we're going to also need to have a list of potential changes you believe might increase the success of your site(s). From now on, we're going to start calling our measure of success a *reward* and our list of potential changes *arms*. The historical reasons for those terms will be described shortly. We don't personally think they're very well-chosen terms, but they're absolutely standard in the academic literature on this topic and will help us make our discussion of algorithms precise.

For now, we want to focus on a different issue: why should we even bother using bandit algorithms to test out new ideas when optimizing websites? Isn't A/B testing already sufficient?

To answer those questions, let's describe the typical A/B testing setup in some detail and then articulate a list of reasons why it may not be ideal.

The Business Scientist: Web-Scale A/B Testing

Most large websites already know a great deal about how to test out new ideas: as described in our short story about Deb Knull, they understand that you can only determine whether a new idea works by performing a controlled experiment.

This style of controlled experimentation is called A/B testing because it typically involves randomly assigning an incoming web user to one of two groups: Group A or Group B. This random assignment of users to groups continues on for a while until the web developer becomes convinced that either Option A is more successful than Option B or, vice versa, that Option B is more successful than Option A. After that, the web developer assigns all future users to the more successful version of the website and closes out the inferior version of the website.

This experimental approach to trying out new ideas has been extremely successful in the past and will continue to be successful in many contexts. So why should we believe that the bandit algorithms described in the rest of this book have anything to offer us?

Answering this question properly requires that we return to the concepts of exploration and exploitation. Standard A/B testing consists of:

- A short period of *pure exploration*, in which you assign equal numbers of users to Groups A and B.

- A long period of *pure exploitation*, in which you send all of your users to the more successful version of your site and never come back to the option that seemed to be inferior.

Why might this be a bad strategy?

- It jumps discretely from exploration into exploitation, when you might be able to smoothly transition between the two.
- During the purely exploratory phase, it wastes resources exploring inferior options in order to gather as much data as possible. But you shouldn't want to gather data about strikingly inferior options.

Bandit algorithms provide solutions to both of these problems: (1) they smoothly decrease the amount of exploring they do over time instead of requiring you to make a sudden jump and (2) they focus your resources during exploration on the better options instead of wasting time on the inferior options that are over-explored during typical A/B testing. In fact, bandit algorithms address both of those concerns is the same way because they gradually fixate on the best available options over time. In the academic literature, this process of settling down on the best available option is called convergence. All good bandit algorithms will eventually converge.

In practice, how important those two types of improvements will be to your business depends a lot on the details of how your business works. But the general framework for thinking about exploration and exploitation provided by bandit algorithms will be useful to you no matter what you end up doing because bandit algorithms subsume A/B testing as a special case. Standard A/B testing describes one extreme case in which you jump from pure exploration to pure exploitation. Bandit algorithms let you operate in the much larger and more interesting space between those two extreme states.

In order to see how bandit algorithms achieve that balance, let's start working with our first algorithm: the epsilon-Greedy algorithm.

CHAPTER 3

The epsilon-Greedy Algorithm

Introducing the epsilon-Greedy Algorithm

To get you started thinking algorithmically about the Explore-Exploit dilemma, we're going to teach you how to code up one of the simplest possible algorithms for trading off exploration and exploitation. This algorithm is called the epsilon-Greedy algorithm. In computer science, a greedy algorithm is an algorithm that always takes whatever action seems best at the present moment, even when that decision might lead to bad long term consequences. The epsilon-Greedy algorithm is almost a greedy algorithm because it generally exploits the best available option, but every once in a while the epsilon-Greedy algorithm explores the other available options. As we'll see, the term epsilon in the algorithm's name refers to the odds that the algorithm explores instead of exploiting.

Let's be more specific. The epsilon-Greedy algorithm works by randomly oscillating between Cynthia's vision of purely randomized experimentation and Bob's instinct to maximize profits. The epsilon-Greedy algorithm is one of the easiest bandit algorithms to understand because it tries to be fair to the two opposite goals of exploration and exploitation by using a mechanism that even a little kid could understand: it just flips a coin. While there are a few details we'll have to iron out to make that statement precise, the big idea behind the epsilon-Greedy algorithm really is that simple: if you flip a coin and it comes up heads, you should explore for a moment. But if the coin comes up tails, you should exploit.

Let's flesh that idea out by continuing on with our example of changing the color of a website's logo to increase revenue. We'll assume that Deb is debating between two colors, green and red, and that she wants to find the one color that maximizes the odds that a new visitor to her site will be converted into a registered user. The epsilon-Greedy algorithm attempts to find the best color logo using the following procedure (shown diagrammatically in Figure 3-1), which is applied to each new potential customer sequentially:

- When a new visitor comes to the site, the algorithm flips a coin that comes up tails with probability epsilon. (If you're not used to thinking in terms of probabilities, the phrase "with probability X" means that something happens 100 * X percent of the time. So saying that a coin comes up tails with probability 0.01 means that it comes up tails 1% of the time.)

- If the coin comes up heads, the algorithm is going to exploit. To exploit, the algorithm looks up the historical conversion rates for both the green and red logos in whatever data source it uses to keep track of things. After determining which color had the highest success rate in the past, the algorithm decides to show the new visitor the color that's been most successful historically.

- If, instead of coming up heads, the coin comes up tails, the algorithm is going to explore. Since exploration involves randomly experimenting with the two colors being considered, the algorithm needs to flip a second coin to choose between them. Unlike the first coin, we'll assume that this second coin comes up head 50% of the time. Once the second coin is flipped, the algorithm can move on with the last step of the procedure:

  — If the second coin comes up heads, show the new visitor the green logo.

  — If the second coin comes up tails, show the new visitor the red logo.

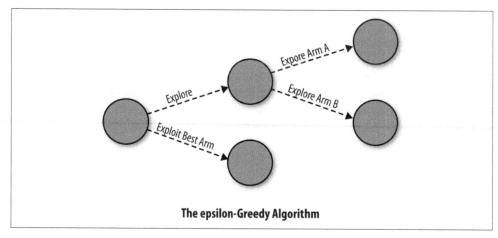

The epsilon-Greedy Algorithm

Figure 3-1. The epsilon-Greedy arm selection process

After letting this algorithm loose on the visitors to a site for a long time, you'll see that it works by oscillating between (A) exploiting the best option that it currently knows about and (B) exploring at random among all of the options available to it. In fact, you know from the definition of the algorithm that:

- With probability `1 - epsilon`, the epsilon-Greedy algorithm *exploits* the best known option.
- With probability `epsilon / 2`, the epsilon-Greedy algorithm *explores* the best known option.
- With probability `epsilon / 2`, the epsilon-Greedy algorithm *explores* the worst known option.

That's it. You now know the entire epsilon-Greedy algorithm. We'll implement the algorithm in Python soon to clarify how'd you deploy this algorithm on a live site, but there's no big ideas missing from the description we just gave. In the next chapter we'll construct a unit-testing framework for the epsilon-Greedy algorithm that will help you start to develop an intuition for how the algorithm would behave in different scenarios.

Describing Our Logo-Choosing Problem Abstractly

What's an Arm?

Before we write code for the epsilon-Greedy algorithm, we need to abstract away from our example in which we wanted to compare a green logo with a red logo. We'll do this in a couple of simple steps that also serve to introduce some of the jargon terms we'll be using throughout the rest of the book.

First, we want to consider the possibility that we have hundreds or thousands of colors to choose from, rather than just two. In general, we're going to assume that we have a fixed set of N different options and that we can enumerate them, so that we can call our green logo *Option 1* and our red logo *Option 2* and any other logo *Option N*. For historical reasons, these options are typically referred to as arms, so we'll talk about *Arm 1* and *Arm 2* and *Arm N* rather than *Option 1*, *Option 2* or *Option N*. But the main idea is the same regardless of the words we choose to employ.

That said, it will help you keep track of these sorts of jargon terms if we explain why the options are typically called arms. This name makes more sense given the original motivations behind the design of the algorithms we're describing in this book: these algorithms were originally invented to explain how an idealized gambler would try to make as much money as possible in a hypothetical casino. In this hypothetical casino, there's only one type of game: a slot machine, which is also sometimes called a one-armed bandit because of its propensity to take your money. While this casino only features slot machines, it could still be an interesting place to visit because there are many different slot machines, each of which has a different payout schedule.

For example, some of the slot machines in this hypothetical casino might pay out $5 on 1 out of 100 pulls, while other machines would pay out $25 on 1 out of 1,000 pulls. For whatever reason, the original mathematicians decided to treat the different slot machines in their thought experiment as if they were one giant slot machine that had many arms. This led them to refer to the options in their problem as arms. It also led them to call this thought experiment the Multiarmed Bandit Problem. To this day, we still call these algorithms bandit algorithms, so knowing the historical names helps to explain why we refer to the options as arms.

What's a Reward?

Now that we've explained what an arm is, we've described one half of the abstract setup of the epsilon-Greedy algorithm. Next, we need to define a *reward*. A reward is simply a measure of success: it might tell us whether a customer clicked on an ad or signed up as a user. What matters is simply that (A) a reward is something quantitative that we can keep of track mathematically and that (B) larger amounts of reward are better than smaller amounts.

What's a Bandit Problem?

Now that we've defined both *arms* and *rewards*, we can describe the abstract idea of a bandit problem that motivates all of the algorithms we'll implement in this book:

- We're facing a complicated slot machine, called a bandit, that has a set of N arms that we can pull on.

- When pulled, any given arm will output a reward. But these rewards aren't reliable, which is why we're gambling: Arm 1 might give us 1 unit of reward only 1% of the time, while Arm 2 might give us 1 unit of reward only 3% of the time. Any specific pull of any specific arm is risky.

- Not only is each pull of an arm risky, we also don't start off knowing what the reward rates are for any of the arms. We have to figure this out experimentally by actually pulling on the unknown arms.

So far the problem we've described in just a problem in statistics: you need to cope with risk by figuring out which arm has the highest average reward. You can calculate the average reward by pulling on each arm a lot of times and computing the mean of the rewards you get back. But a real bandit problem is more complicated and also more realistic.

What makes a bandit problem special is that we only receive a small amount of the information about the rewards from each arm. Specifically:

- We only find out about the reward that was given out by the arm we actually pulled. Whichever arm we pull, we miss out on information about the other arms that we didn't pull. Just like in real life, you only learn about the path you took and not the paths you could have taken.

In fact, the situation is worse than that. Not only do we get only partial feedback about the wisdom of our past decisions, we're literally falling behind every time we don't make a good decision:

- Every time we experiment with an arm that isn't the best arm, we lose reward because we could, *at least in principle*, have pulled on a better arm.

The full Multiarmed Bandit Problem is defined by the five features above. Any algorithm that offers you a proposed solution to the Multiarmed Bandit Problem must give you a rule for selecting arms in some sequence. And this rule has to balance out your competing desires to (A) learn about new arms and (B) earn as much reward as possible by pulling on arms you already know are good choices.

Implementing the epsilon-Greedy Algorithm

Now that we've defined a Multiarmed Bandit Problem abstractly, we can give you a clear description of the general epsilon-Greedy algorithm that's easy to implement in Python. We'll do this in a few steps because that will let us define a very general interface for bandit algorithms that we'll be using throughout this book.

First, we define a class of objects that represents an epsilon-Greedy algorithm as it's going to be deployed in the wild. This class will encapsulate the following pieces of information:

epsilon
: This will be a floating point number that tells us the frequency with which we should explore one of the available arms. If we set epsilon = 0.1, then we'll explore the available arms on 10% of our pulls.

counts
: A vector of integers of length N that tells us how many times we've played each of the N arms available to us in the current bandit problem. If there are two arms, Arm 1 and Arm 2, which have both been played twice, then we'll set counts = [2, 2].

values

A vector of floating point numbers that defines the average amount of reward we've gotten when playing each of the N arms available to us. If Arm 1 gave us 1 unit of reward on one play and 0 on another play, while Arm 2 gave us 0 units of reward on both plays, then we'll set values = [0.5, 0.0].

Putting these pieces together into a proper class definition, we end up with the following snippet of code:

```
class EpsilonGreedy():
  def __init__(self, epsilon, counts, values):
    self.epsilon = epsilon
    self.counts = counts
    self.values = values
    return
```

Because the epsilon-Greedy algorithm's behavior is very strongly controlled by the settings of both counts and values, we also provide explicit initialization methods that let you reset these variables to their proper blank slate states before letting the algorithms loose:

```
def initialize(self, n_arms):
  self.counts = [0 for col in range(n_arms)]
  self.values = [0.0 for col in range(n_arms)]
  return
```

Now that we have a class that represents all of the information that the epsilon-Greedy algorithm needs to keep track of about each of the arms, we need to define two types of behaviors that any algorithm for solving the Multiarmed Bandit Problem should provide:

select_arm

Every time we have to make a choice about which arm to pull, we want to be able to simply make a call to our favorite algorithm and have it tell us the numeric name of the arm we should pull. Throughout this book, all of the bandit algorithms will implement a select_arm method that is called without any arguments and which returns the index of the next arm to pull.

update

After we pull an arm, we get a reward signal back from our system. (In the next chapter, we'll describe a testing framework we've built that simulates these rewards so that we can debug our bandit algorithms.) We want to update our algorithm's beliefs about the quality of the arm we just chose by providing this reward information. Throughout this book, all of the bandit algorithms handle this by providing an update function that takes as arguments (1) an algorithm object, (2) the numeric index of the most recently chosen arm and (3) the reward received from choosing that arm. The update method will take this information and make the relevant changes to the algorithm's evaluation of all of the arms.

Keeping in mind that general framework for behaviors that we expect a bandit algorithm to provide, let's walk through the specific definition of these two functions for the epsilon-Greedy algorithm. First, we'll implement `select_arm`:

```python
def ind_max(x):
  m = max(x)
  return x.index(m)

def select_arm(self):
  if random.random() > self.epsilon:
    return ind_max(self.values)
  else:
    return random.randrange(len(self.values))
```

As you can see, the epsilon-Greedy algorithm handles selecting an arm in two parts: (1) we flip a coin to see if we'll choose the best arm we know about and then (2) if the coin comes up tails, we'll select an arm completely at random. In Python, we've implemented this by checking if a randomly generated number is greater than epsilon. If so, our algorithm selects the arm whose cached value according to the values field is highest; otherwise, it selects an arm at random.

These few lines of code completely describe the epsilon-Greedy algorithm's solution to the Bandit problem: it explores some percentage of the time and otherwise chooses the arm it thinks is best. But, to understand which arm our epsilon-Greedy algorithm considers best, we need to define the update function. Let's do that now, then explain why the procedure we've chosen is reasonable:

```python
def update(self, chosen_arm, reward):
  self.counts[chosen_arm] = self.counts[chosen_arm] + 1
  n = self.counts[chosen_arm]

  value = self.values[chosen_arm]
  new_value = ((n - 1) / float(n)) * value + (1 / float(n)) * reward
  self.values[chosen_arm] = new_value
  return
```

Looking at this code, we see that the update function first increments the counts field that records the number of times we've played each of the arms for this bandit problem to reflect the chosen arm. Then it finds the current estimated value of the chosen arm. If this is our first experience ever with the chosen arm, we set the estimated value directly to the reward we just received from playing that arm. If we had played the arm in the past, we update the estimated value of the chosen arm to be a weighted average of the previously estimated value and the reward we just received. This weighting is important, because it means that single observations mean less and less to the algorithm when we already have a lot of experience with any specific option. The specific weighting we've chosen is designed to insure that the estimated value is exactly equal to the average of the rewards we've gotten from each arm.

We suspect that it will not be obvious to many readers why this update rule computes a running average. To convince you why this works, consider the standard definition of an average:

```
def average(values):
  result = 0.0
  for value in values:
    result = result + value

  return result / len(values)
```

Instead of doing the division at the end, we could do it earlier on:

```
def average(values):
  result = 0.0
  n = float(len(values))
  for value in values:
    result = result + value / n

  return result
```

This alternative implementation looks much more like the update rule we're using for the epsilon-Greedy algorithm. The core insight you need to have to fully see the relationship between our update rule and this method for computing averages is this: the average of the first n - 1 values is just their sum divided by n - 1. So multiplying that average by (n - 1) / n will give you exactly the value that result has in the code above when you've processed the first n - 1 entries in values. If that explanation is not clear to you, we suggest that you print out the value of result at each step in the loop until you see the pattern we're noting.

 We're making a point now about how to compute averages online because much of the behavior of bandit algorithms in practice is driven by this rule for calculating averages. Near the end of the book we'll talk about alternative weighting schemes that you might use instead of computing averages. Those alternative weighting schemes are very important when the arms you're playing can shift their rewards over time.

But for now, let's focus on what we've done so far. Taken all together, the class definition we gave for the EpsilonGreedy class and the definitions of the select_arm and update methods for that class fully define our implementation of the epsilon-Greedy algorithm. In order to let you try out the algorithm before deploying it, we're going to spend time in the next chapter setting up a type of unit-testing framework for bandit algorithms.

But first let's think critically about the strengths and weaknesses of the algorithm we've defined by thinking in our armchairs about the behavior of the functions we've just defined. By thinking about where we've made judgment calls in defining our algorithm, we can come up with a set of principles that we'll eventually be able to use to design other algorithms for solving the Multiarmed Bandit Problem.

Thinking Critically about the epsilon-Greedy Algorithm

Before we do anything else, let's demonstrate that the epsilon-Greedy algorithm can be configured to behave exactly in the way that Cynthia suggested, which involved completely random experimentation like you'd do during traditional A/B testing. After we show that you can configure the epsilon-Greedy algorithm to behave like A/B testing, we'll show you that the epsilon-Greedy algorithm can also be configured to behave exactly like the profit-maximization rule that Bob hoped Deb would settle upon after her experimental phase was over.

Setting up the epsilon-Greedy algorithm to achieve either of these goals is surprisingly easy: Cynthia's original experimental design involves assigning each visitor to Deb's website to one of two colors completely at random, which is exactly how the epsilon-Greedy algorithm behaves if it knows about 2 arms and has set `epsilon = 1.0`. We can do that by simplying instantiating our `EpsilonGreedy` class with the right parameters:

```
algo = EpsilonGreedy(1.0, [])
initialize(algo, 2)
```

Bob's rule for profit-maximization is also a single line:

```
algo.epsilon = 0.0
```

Those three lines fully describe Cynthia and Bob's approaches, which are literally the two most extreme ways that you can configure the epsilon-Greedy algorithm. Cynthia wanted to do nothing but exploration, while Bob wanted to do nothing but exploitation. We can often do better by choosing a middle ground position. To see why, let's think carefully about the implications of the decision to set `epsilon` to either of the specific values proposed by Cynthia and Bob.

If we set `epsilon = 1.0`, the algorithm will always choose among the different arms completely at random. This will provide you with a lot of data about both color logos and will produce very clean data, because all of the arms will have equal amounts of data and there won't be any lurking confounds that make it hard to understand why you got the results you got. If you're a traditionally trained scientist, this type of random experimentation will seem like a great approach. But it can lose a lot of money when you're a business, because it means you're as likely to try a bad idea as you are to try a good idea.

Or, to put the point another way: if you run a business, you *should not* want to accumulate a lot of data about bad options. You should want to only gather data about options that could plausibly be worth implementing. This was Bob's criticism of Cynthia's plan: setting epsilon = 1.0 wastes resources acquiring data about bad options. Returning to our example of logos, if you select between the two colors completely at random, you've decided that you'll show your customers your worst logo exactly as often as your best logo.

But Bob's main response to this concern wasn't ideal. If you eventually set epsilon = 0.0, it's true that you'll stop wasting time on bad options. But you'll never be able to learn about new options ever again. If the world changes and you don't provide your company with any mechanism for learning about the changes in the world, your company will be left behind. Cynthia's scientific approach explored the options available to her willy-nilly, but Bob's short-sighted proposal would leave the company ossified, unable to adapt to a changing world and incapable of trying out new ideas.

Thankfully, there's no reason you need to operate at either of these two extremes. Instead of moving from one period of completely random experimentation to another period of absolutely greedy selection of the so-called best option, the epsilon-Greedy algorithm lets you be more gradual. You could, for example, set epsilon = 0.1 and leave the algorithm running forever. In many situations, this might be a better option that either Cynthia or Bob's plans.

But there are weaknesses with this approach as well. The first weakness is that, as you get more certain which of your two logo designs is best, this tendency to explore the worse design a full 5% of the time will become more wasteful. In the jargon of bandit algorithms, you'll be over-exploring. And there's another problem with a fixed 10% exploration rule: at the start of your experimentation, you'll choose options that you don't know much about far more rarely than you'd like to because you only try new options 10% of the time.

So there are many ways that the epsilon-Greedy algorithm could be better. In the rest of this book, we'll describe other algorithms that can improve on the epsilon-Greedy algorithm. But for now we'd like to help you set up a testbed for trying out the epsilon-Greedy algorithm so that you can see how it really works in action.

To do this, we'll provide a sort of unit-testing framework for bandit algorithms that exploits an idea developed during World War II called Monte Carlo simulation. The main idea is that we can use a random number generator to simulate what might happen if you deployed an algorithm in the wild under lots of different circumstances. We'll work through a specific example while building up our general framework in the next chapter.

CHAPTER 4

Debugging Bandit Algorithms

Monte Carlo Simulations Are Like Unit Tests for Bandit Algorithms

Even though the last chapter contained a full implementation of the epsilon-Greedy algorithm, it was still a very abstract discussion because the algorithm was never run. The reason for that is simple: unlike standard machine learning tools, bandit algorithms aren't simply black-box functions you can call to process the data you have lying around — bandit algorithms have to actively select which data you should acquire and analyze that data in real-time. Indeed, bandit algorithms exemplify two types of learning that are not present in standard ML examples: *active learning*, which refers to algorithms that actively select which data they should receive; and *online learning*, which refers to algorithms that analyze data in real-time and provide results on the fly.

This means that there is a complicated feedback cycle in every bandit algorithm: as shown in Figure 4-1, the behavior of the algorithm depends on the data it sees, but the data the algorithm sees depends on the behavior of the algorithm. Debugging a bandit algorithm is therefore substantially more complicated than debugging a straight machine learning algorithm that isn't doing active learning. You can't just feed a bandit algorithm data: you have to turn it loose somewhere to see how it might behave in production. Of course, doing this on your own site could be very risky: you don't want to unleash untested code on a live site.

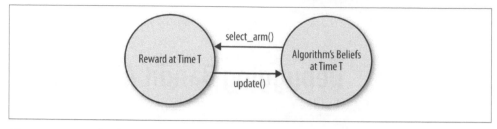

Figure 4-1. Bandit data and bandit analysis are inseparable

In order to solve both of these problems, we're going to use an alternative to standard unit-testing that's appropriate for testing bandit algorithms. This alternative is called Monte Carlo simulations. The name comes from World War II, when scientists tested how weaponry and other systems might behave by using simple computers equipped with a random number generator.

For our purposes, a Monte Carlo simulation will let our implementation of a bandit algorithm actively make decisions about which data it will receive, because our simulations will be able to provide simulated data in real-time to the algorithm for analysis. In short, we're going to deal with the feedback cycle shown earlier by coding up both our bandit algorithm and a simulation of the bandit's arms that the algorithm has to select between. The two pieces of code then work together to generate an example of how the algorithm might really function in production.

Because each simulation is powered by random numbers, the results are noisy. For that reason, you'll want to run lots of simulations. Thankfully, modern computers, unlike those used in World War II, are well up to the task. As you'll see in a moment, we can easily simulate 100,000's of runs of a bandit algorithm to develop an intuition for its behavior in different settings. This is arguably far more important than understanding any specific bandit algorithm, so please don't skip this section of the book.

Simulating the Arms of a Bandit Problem

In order to reasonably simulate what might happen if you were to deploy an epsilon-Greedy algorithm in production, we need to set up some hypothetical arms. For this book, we're going to focus on a very simple type of simulated arm that's easy to implement correctly. This hypothetical arm will let us simulate settings like:

- *Optimizing click-through rates for ads*: Every time we show someone an ad, we'll imagine that there's a fixed probability that they'll click on the ad. The bandit algorithm will then estimate this probability and try to decide on a strategy for showing ads that maximizes the click-through rate.

- *Conversion rates for new users*: Every time a new visitor comes to our site who isn't already a registered user, we'll imagine that there's a fixed probability that they'll register as a user after seeing the landing page. We'll then estimate this probability and try to decide on a strategy for maximizing our conversion rate.

Our simulated arm is going to be called a Bernoulli arm. Calling this type of an arm a Bernoulli arm is just a jargony way of saying that we're dealing with an arm that rewards you with a value of 1 some percentage of the time and rewards you with a value of 0 the rest of the time. This 0/1 framework is a very simple way to simulate situations like click-throughs or user signups: the potential user arrives at your site; you select an arm for them in which you, for example, show them one specific color logo; finally, they either do sign up for the site (and give you reward 1) or they don't (and give you reward 0). If 2% of people who see a red logo sign up and 5% of people who see a green logo sign up, then you can abstract away the details and talk about two arms: one arm outputs 1 unit of reward 2% of the time, the other arm outputs 1 unit of reward 5% of the time. This situation is what we call a Bernoulli arm. We implement it in Python as follows:

```python
class BernoulliArm():
  def __init__(self, p):
    self.p = p

  def draw(self):
    if random.random() > self.p:
      return 0.0
    else:
      return 1.0
```

First, there's a class called `BernoulliArm` that has a single field, p, which tells us the probability of getting a reward of 1 from that arm. Second, there's a method, `draw`, that, when called, produces 1 unit of reward with probability p. That's the entirety of our abstract way of thinking about click-throughs and so on. Amazingly enough, this provides enough material for a very powerful simulation framework.

The only big thing that's missing from this approach is that we typically have to work with many arms, so we'll need to set up an array of Arm objects. For example, we could do the following:

```python
means = [0.1, 0.1, 0.1, 0.1, 0.9]
n_arms = len(means)
random.shuffle(means)
arms = map(lambda (mu): BernoulliArm(mu), means)
```

This will set up an array that contains 5 arms. 4 of them output reward 10% of the time, while the best of them outputs a reward 90% of the time. This is a very black-and-white situation that you won't see in the real world, but that means that it's a nice starting point for testing our algorithms. We'll be using it throughout the rest of this book.

To try out our Bernoulli arms, you might call draw a few times on some of the elements of our array as follows:

```
arms[0].draw()
arms[1].draw()
arms[2].draw()
arms[2].draw()
arms[3].draw()
arms[2].draw()
arms[4].draw()
```

A typical output from this might look like:

```
>>> arms[0].draw()
1.0
>>> arms[1].draw()
0.0
>>> arms[2].draw()
0.0
>>> arms[2].draw()
0.0
>>> arms[3].draw()
0.0
>>> arms[2].draw()
0.0
>>> arms[4].draw()
0.0
```

That should give you some sense of how this setup works. Our Multiarmed Bandit problem gets represented as an array of arm objects, each of which implements a draw method that simulates playing that specific arm.

With that in place, we're almost ready to start experimenting with the epsilon-Greedy algorithm. But before we do that, we're going to set up a very generic framework for testing an algorithm. This framework is described entirely by the test_algorithm function shown below and will be the only testing tool needed for the rest of this book. Let's go through it now:

```
def test_algorithm(algo, arms, num_sims, horizon):
    chosen_arms = [0.0 for i in range(num_sims * horizon)]
    rewards = [0.0 for i in range(num_sims * horizon)]
    cumulative_rewards = [0.0 for i in range(num_sims * horizon)]
    sim_nums = [0.0 for i in range(num_sims * horizon)]
    times = [0.0 for i in range(num_sims * horizon)]

    for sim in range(num_sims):
        sim = sim + 1
        algo.initialize(len(arms))

        for t in range(horizon):
            t = t + 1
            index = (sim - 1) * horizon + t - 1
```

```
        sim_nums[index] = sim
        times[index] = t

        chosen_arm = algo.select_arm()
        chosen_arms[index] = chosen_arm

        reward = arms[chosen_arms[index]].draw()
        rewards[index] = reward

        if t == 1:
          cumulative_rewards[index] = reward
        else:
          cumulative_rewards[index] = cumulative_rewards[index - 1] + reward

        algo.update(chosen_arm, reward)

    return [sim_nums, times, chosen_arms, rewards, cumulative_rewards]
```

How does this framework work?

- We pass in a few objects:
  - A bandit algorithm that we want to test.
  - An array of arms we want to simulate draws from.
  - A fixed number of simultations to run to average over the noise in each simulation.
  - The number of times each algorithm is allowed to pull on arms during each simulation. Any algorithm that's not terrible will eventually learn which arm is best; the interesting thing to study in a simulation is whether an algorithm does well when it only has 100 (or 100,000) tries to find the best arm.
- The framework then uses these objects to run many independent simulations. For each of these, it:
  - Initializes the bandit algorithm's settings from scratch so that it has no prior knowledge about which arm is best.
  - Loops over opportunities to pull an arm. On each step of this loop, it:
    - Calls select_arm to see which arm the algorithm chooses.
    - Calls draw on that arm to simulate the result of pulling that arm.
    - Records the amount of reward received by the algorithm and then calls update to let the algorithm process that new piece of information.
- Finally, the testing framework returns a data set that tells us for each simulation which arm was chosen and how well the algorithm did at each point in time. In the code directory associated with this book, there are R scripts that plot out the performance to give you a feel for how these algorithms perform. We won't step through that code in detail in this book, but it is available online in the same GitHub repos-

itory as you're using for all of the other code for this book. Instead of walking through our graphics code, we'll show you plots that describe what happens during our simulations and try to make sure you understand the main qualitative properties you should be looking for in the data you'll get from your own simulations.

To show you how to use this testing framework, we need to pass in a specific algorithm and a specific set of arms. In the code below, we show you what happens when applying the epsilon-Greedy algorithm we implemented earlier against the five Bernoulli arms we defined just a moment ago. For simplicity, we've reproduced all of the necessary code below, including redefining the five Bernoulli arms:

```
execfile("core.py")

import random

random.seed(1)
means = [0.1, 0.1, 0.1, 0.1, 0.9]
n_arms = len(means)
random.shuffle(means)
arms = map(lambda (mu): BernoulliArm(mu), means)
print("Best arm is " + str(ind_max(means)))

f = open("algorithms/epsilon_greedy/standard_results.tsv", "w")

for epsilon in [0.1, 0.2, 0.3, 0.4, 0.5]:
  algo = EpsilonGreedy(epsilon, [], [])
  algo.initialize(n_arms)
  results = test_algorithm(algo, arms, 5000, 250)
  for i in range(len(results[0])):
      f.write(str(epsilon) + "\t")
      f.write("\t".join([str(results[j][i]) for j in range(len(results))]) + "\n")

f.close()
```

Analyzing Results from a Monte Carlo Study

With the results from our simulation study in hand, we can analyze our data in several different ways to assess the performance of our algorithms.

Approach 1: Track the Probability of Choosing the Best Arm

The first analytic approach, and certainly the simplest, is to keep track of the odds that our algorithm selects the best arm at any given point in time. We need to work with odds for two different reasons: (1) the algorithm uses randomization when choosing which arm to pull and may therefore not select the best arm even after it's learned which arm is best and (2) the rewards that the algorithm receives are random as well. For those reasons, there is always a chance that the algorithm will not make the best decision on any specific trial.

As such, we'll explicitly calculate the probability of selecting the best arm by estimating the percentage of times in our simulations when the algorithm chose the best arm. If the probability that the algorithm picks the best arm doesn't go up over time, then we don't really have any evidence that our algorithm is learning anything about the values of the arms. Thankfully, the results shown in Figure 4-2, which split up the data by the value of epsilon, show that our algorithm does indeed learn no matter how we set epsilon.

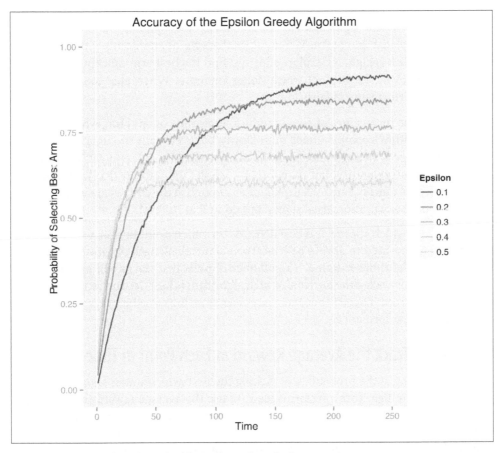

Figure 4-2. How often does the algorithm select the best arm?

Let's step through this graph carefully to understand its message. Before we say anything else, let's be possibly pedantically clear about the axes:

- The x-axis shows the number of times the algorithm has been able to pull on any of the five arms that are available.
- The y-axis shows the probability that the algorithm, when we called `se lect_arm()`, chose the best of the five arms at each point in time.
- The actual values of the curves are the averages across the 5,000 simulations we ran to estimate the algorithm's performance. We needed to run 5,000 simulations to get around the amount of noise in each simulation caused by using a random number generator in our simulations.

The first thing you should notice is that each setting of `epsilon` produces a separate curve. The curves with high values of `epsilon` go up very quickly, but then peak out. That's a given, because the epsilon-Greedy algorithms choose randomly with probability epsilon. If `epsilon` is high, we explore a lot and find the best arm quickly, but then we keep exploring even after it's not worth doing anymore. When `epsilon` is high, our system's peak performance is fairly low.

In contrast to the high values of `epsilon`, the lowest value of `epsilon`, which was `0.1`, causes the algorithm to explore much more slowly, but eventually the algorithm reaches a much higher peak performance level. In many ways, the different settings of `epsi lon` embody the Explore-Exploit trade-off as a whole: the settings that lead to lots of exploration learn quickly, but don't exploit often enough at the end; whereas the settings that lead to little exploration learn slowly, but do well at the end.

As you can see, which approach is best depends on which point in time you're looking at. This is why we need to always be concerned about the length of time we intend to leave a bandit algorithm running. The number of pulls that the bandit algorithm has left to it is typically called the horizon. Which algorithm is best depends strongly on the length of the horizon. That will become more clear as we look at other ways of measuring our algorithm's performance.

Approach 2: Track the Average Reward at Each Point in Time

Instead of looking at the probability of picking the best arm, another simple approach to measuring our algorithm's performance is to use the average reward that our algorithm receives on each trial. When there are many arms similar to the best, each of which is just a little worse than the best, this average reward approach is a much better method of analysis than our approach using probabilities of selecting the best arm. You can see the results for this alternative analysis in Figure 4-3.

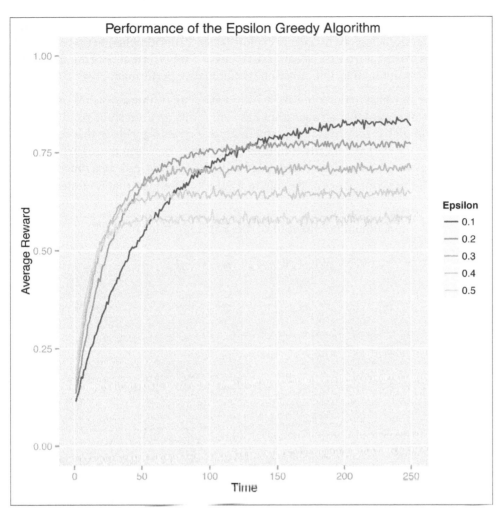

Figure 4-3. How much reward does the algorithm earn on average?

In this specific case, the results are quite similar because (A) the rewards are so far apart and because (B) the rewards are all 0's or 1's. But these types of metrics can differ much more in other settings. Your mileage may vary.

Approach 3: Track the Cumulative Reward at Each Point in Time

Ultimately, there's something lacking in both of the approaches we've taken: they're too narrowly focused on the performance of the algorithm at each fixed point in time and don't give us a gestalt picture of the lifetime performance of our algorithm. This myopic focus on each point in time in isolation is unfair to versions of the epsilon-Greedy algorithm in which epsilon is large, because these algorithms, by definition, explore worse options more frequently than algorithms for which epsilon is low. This is a sacrifice they intentionally make in order to explore faster. To decide whether that increased exploration is worth the trouble, we shouldn't focus on the performance of the algorithm at any specific point in time, but rather on its cumulative performance over time.

To do that, we can analyze the cumulative reward of our algorithms, which is simply the total amount of reward that an algorithm has won for us up until some fixed point in time. This cumulative reward is important, because it treats algorithms that do a lot of exploration at the start as a means of finding the best available arm more fairly. As you can see in Figure 4-4, an analysis based on cumulative rewards leads to a much cleaner assessment of the performance of the different values of epsilon that we tested.

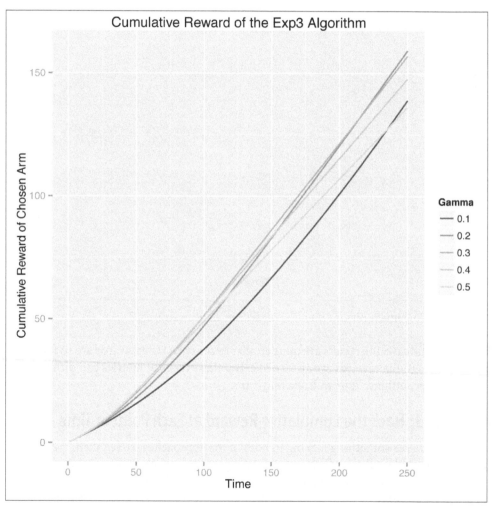

Figure 4-4. How much reward has the algorithm earned by trial t?

In fact, looking at the cumulative results, you can see that curves for the low value of epsilon = 0.1 and the high value of epsilon = 0.5 intersect after about 130 rounds: before then, it was good to have explored a lot, but after then it was better to have been able to exploit more consistently once the algorithm had found the best arm.

That said, all of our figures convey the same basic message: the epsilon-Greedy algorithm does eventually figure out which arm is best no matter how epsilon is set. But the length of time required to figure our which arm is best depends a lot on the value of epsilon. What's appropriate for you depends on how long you intend to run your algorithm and how different the arms you're testing will be. To see how the epsilon-Greedy algorithm might behave for your website, you should use our testing framework to simulate the types of click-through rates you're used to seeing. We suggest some of these in a list of exercises below.

Exercises

In order to really build a feel for the epsilon-Greedy algorithm, you need to see how it behaves under a variety of circumstances. To do that, you should try out the following exercises:

- Use a different number of arms than the five arms we've been working with. See how epsilon-Greedy behaves if there are 2 arms and then see how it behaves if there are 200 arms.

- Change the probabilities of reward from the Bernoulli arms. How does epsilon-Greedy behave if all of the probabilities are close to 0.0? How does it behave it all of the probabilities are close to 1.0? How does it behave when the probabilities for different arms are similar? How does it behave when they're far apart?

After seeing how the standard epsilon-Greedy algorithm behaves, we'd also encourage you to experiment with trying to modify the epsilon-Greedy to be a little better. There are two specific tricks you will find are worth exploring:

- Change the initialization rules for the values fields. Instead of assuming that every arm has value 0.0 (which amounts to extreme pessimism about unfamiliar arms), try assuming instead that every arm has value 1.0 at the start. How does this change the behavior of the algorithm on different problems?

- Build a modified version of the epsilon-Greedy algorithm that can change the value of epsilon over time, so that epsilon is high at the start and low at the end of a simulation. This change from lots of exploration to little exploration is called annealing and will come up again in the next chapter. Implementing annealing for the epsilon-Greedy algorithm is particularly informative about the weaknesses of the standard epsilon-Greedy algorithm.

- A more involved problem you can work on is to devise an alternative test for evaluating the performance of the epsilon-Greedy algorithm. In this alternative setup, you should keep track of the peformance of the algorithm only on trials when it is trying to exploit. This requires that you store more information during each simulation than we are currently storing, but it can help you to build up an intuition for how the epsilon-Greedy algorithm behaves.

CHAPTER 5

The Softmax Algorithm

Introducing the Softmax Algorithm

If you've completed the exercises for Chapter 2, you should have discovered that there's an obvious problem with the epsilon-Greedy algorithm: it explores options completely at random without any concern about their merits. For example, in one scenario (call it Scenario A), you might have two arms, one of which rewards you 10% of the time and the other rewards you 13% of the time. In Scenario B, the two arms might reward you 10% of the time and 99% of the time. In both of these scenarios, the probability that the epsilon-Greedy algorithm explores the worse arm is exactly the same (it's epsilon / 2), despite the inferior arm in Scenario B being, in relative terms, much worse than the inferior arm in Scenario A.

This is a problem for several reasons:

- If the difference in reward rates between two arms is small, you'll need to explore a lot more often than 10% of the time to correctly determine which of the two options is actually better.

- In contrast, if the difference is large, you need to explore a lot less than 10% of the time to correctly estimate the better of the two options. For that reason, you'll end up losing a lot of reward by exploring an unambiguously inferior option in this case. When we first described the epsilon-Greedy algorithm, we said that we wouldn't set epsilon = 1.0 precisely so that we wouldn't waste time on inferior options, but, if the difference between two arms is large enough, we end up wasting time on inferior options simply because the epsilon-Greedy algorithm always explores completely at random.

Putting these two points together, it seems clear that there's a qualitative property missing from the epsilon-Greedy algorithm. We need to make our bandit algorithm care about the known differences between the estimated values of the arms when our algorithm decides which arm to explore. We need *structured exploration* rather than the *haphazard exploration* that the epsilon-Greedy algorithm provides.

The first algorithm we'll describe that takes this structural information into account is called the Softmax algorithm. The Softmax algorithm tries to cope with arms differing in estimated value by explicitly incorporating information about the reward rates of the available arms into its method for choosing which arm to select when it explores.

You can get an initial intuition for how the Softmax algorithm handles this problem by imagining that you choose each arm in proportion to its estimated value. Suppose that you have two arms, A and B. Now imagine that, based on your past experiences, these two arms have had two different rates of success: rA and rB. With those assumptions, the most naive possible implementation of a Softmax-like algorithm would have you choose Arm A with probability rA / (rA + rB) and Arm B with probability rB / (rA + rB). In code, this proportional approach would look like:

```
def categorical_draw(probs):
  z = random.random()
  cum_prob = 0.0
  for i in range(len(probs)):
    prob = probs[i]
    cum_prob += prob
    if cum_prob > z:
      return i

  return len(probs) - 1

def select_arm(self):
  z = sum(self.values)
  probs = [v / z for v in self.values]
  return categorical_draw(probs)
```

In practice, this very naive algorithm isn't something people actually use. To reconstruct the algorithm people actually use, we need to make two changes to it.

First, we will calculate a different scale for reward rates by exponentiating our estimates of rA and rB. Using this new scale, we will choose Arm A with probability exp(rA) / (exp(rA) + exp(rB)) and Arm B with probability exp(rB) / (exp(rA) + exp(rB)). This naive exponential rescaling has the virtue of not behaving strangely if you someone used negative numbers as rates of success, since the call to exp will turn any negative numbers into positive numbers and insure that the negative numbers in the denominator of these fractions can't cancel out any positive numbers that may be found in the denominator.

More importantly, this exponentiation trick brings us very close to the full Softmax algorithm. In fact, plain exponential rescaling gives us the Softmax algorithm if you hardcoded one of the configurable parameters that the standard Softmax algorithm possesses. This additional parameter is a different sort of scaling factor than the exponentiation we just introduced.

This new type of scaling factor is typically called a temperature parameter based on an analogy with physics in which systems at high temperatures tend to behave randomly, while they take on more structure at low temperatures. In fact, the full Softmax algorithm is closely related to a concept called the Boltzmann distribution in physics, which is used to describe how groups of particles behave.

We'll call this new temperature parameter tau. We introduce tau to produce the following new algorithm:

- At time T, select one of the two arms with probabilities computed as follows:
  - exp(rA / tau) / (exp(rA / tau) + exp(rB / tau))
  - exp(rB / tau) / (exp(rA / tau) + exp(rB / tau))
- For whichever arm you picked, update your estimate of the mean using the same update rule we used for the epsilon-Greedy algorithm.

Implementing the Softmax Algorithm

Putting these new ideas together, we get the following code for the full Softmax algorithm:

```
import math
import random

def categorical_draw(probs):
  z = random.random()
  cum_prob = 0.0
  for i in range(len(probs)):
    prob = probs[i]
    cum_prob += prob
    if cum_prob > z:
      return i

  return len(probs) - 1

class Softmax:
  def __init__(self, temperature, counts, values):
    self.temperature = temperature
    self.counts = counts
    self.values = values
    return
```

```
def initialize(self, n_arms):
  self.counts = [0 for col in range(n_arms)]
  self.values = [0.0 for col in range(n_arms)]
  return

def select_arm(self):
  z = sum([math.exp(v / self.temperature) for v in self.values])
  probs = [math.exp(v / self.temperature) / z for v in self.values]
  return categorical_draw(probs)

def update(self, chosen_arm, reward):
  self.counts[chosen_arm] = self.counts[chosen_arm] + 1
  n = self.counts[chosen_arm]

  value = self.values[chosen_arm]
  new_value = ((n - 1) / float(n)) * value + (1 / float(n)) * reward
  self.values[chosen_arm] = new_value
  return
```

Now that we have the Softmax algorithm fully described and implemented, we should spend some time discussing what the temperature parameter tau does. It's easiest to think of tau as letting us shift the behavior of the Softmax algorithm along a continuum defined by two extreme ways to select arms. At one extreme, we set tau = 0.0. This will give us a fully deterministic choice of the arm that has the highest estimated value. At the other extreme, we set tau = Inf, which gives us purely random exploration like we got out of the epsilon-Greedy algorithm. The reason this tau parameter is called a temperature parameter is that its effect on the selection of arms is like the effect of temperatures on atoms in traditional physics: at low temperatures, atoms will behave orderly and produce solids, but at high temperatures, they behavior randomly and will produce gases. Like atoms, the Softmax algorithm at low temperatures behaves orderly, while it behaves essentially randomly at high temperatures.

Now that you understand the basic idea of the Softmax algorithm, let's try it out in the same simulated deployment scenarios in which we tested the epsilon-greedy algorithm before.

```
execfile("core.py")

import random

random.seed(1)
means = [0.1, 0.1, 0.1, 0.1, 0.9]
n_arms = len(means)
random.shuffle(means)
arms = map(lambda (mu): BernoulliArm(mu), means)
print("Best arm is " + str(ind_max(means)))

f = open("algorithms/softmax/standard_softmax_results.tsv", "w")
```

```
for temperature in [0.1, 0.2, 0.3, 0.4, 0.5]:
  algo = Softmax(temperature, [], [])
  algo.initialize(n_arms)
  results = test_algorithm(algo, arms, 5000, 250)
  for i in range(len(results[0])):
      f.write(str(temperature) + "\t")
      f.write("\t".join([str(results[j][i]) for j in range(len(results))]) + "\n")

f.close()
```

Measuring the Performance of the Softmax Algorithm

How does the Softmax algorithm do? Again we're going to use our simulation tools. We reproduce all of the code for our new simulations below:

```
execfile("core.py")

import random

random.seed(1)
means = [0.1, 0.1, 0.1, 0.1, 0.9]
n_arms = len(means)
random.shuffle(means)
arms = map(lambda (mu): BernoulliArm(mu), means)
print("Best arm is " + str(ind_max(means)))

f = open("algorithms/softmax/standard_softmax_results.tsv", "w")

for temperature in [0.1, 0.2, 0.3, 0.4, 0.5]:
  algo = Softmax(temperature, [], [])
  algo.initialize(n_arms)
  results = test_algorithm(algo, arms, 5000, 250)
  for i in range(len(results[0])):
      f.write(str(temperature) + "\t")
      f.write("\t".join([str(results[j][i]) for j in range(len(results))]) + "\n")

f.close()
```

As before, we'll walk through some analyses of the results using simple graphics. While we're interested in comparing the Softmax algorithm with the epsilon-Greedy algorithm, we're going to hold off on making full comparisons between algorithms until the next chapter.

For now we can just eyeball results from our Softmax simulations to get a sense of how it performs relative to the expectations set by the epsilon-Greedy algorithm. As we did with the epsilon-Greedy algorithm, we'll start by plotting the probability that the Softmax algorithm selects the best arm. The results are shown in Figure 5-1.

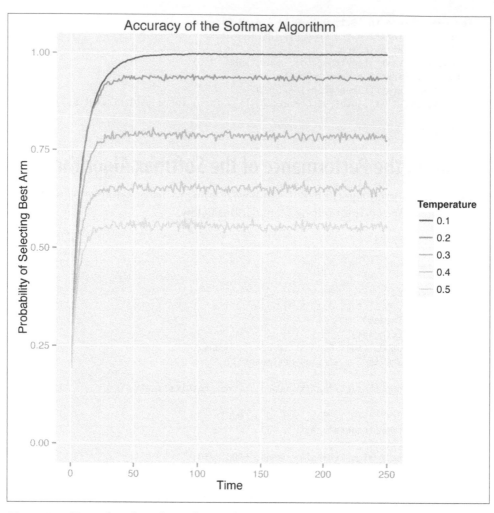

Figure 5-1. How often does the Softmax algorithm select the best arm?

Looking at the probability that the softmax algorithm selects the right arm, we see that it starts to select the right arm 100% of the time if we wait long enough. This is a big improvement over the epsilon-Greedy algorithm, which never got past the intrinsic errors caused by the purely random exploration strategy it used. In our standard test case, there is one standout arm and the softmax algorithm is able to find it and exploit it far more effectively than the epsilon-Greedy algorithm.

We see the same results looking at the average reward rates plotted in Figure 5-2, except that the rewards are capped at 0.9 instead of 1.0 because 0.9 is the expected rate of reward associated with the best arm in our test suite.

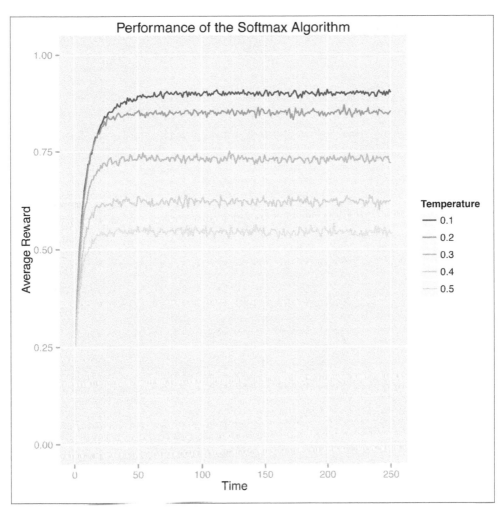

Figure 5-2. How much reward does the Softmax algorithm earn on average?

Finally, we can get more insight into the different temperature settings we can use by looking at the cumulative rewards earned as shown in Figure 5-3. In this figure, we can see that the lowest temperature setting we used, 0.1, gives us the best results nearly right from the start. This is typical in settings in which there are clear differences between arms. It's much less likely that the low level of exploration we're seeing from the 0.1 temperature Softmax will be ideal if the arms are closer together.

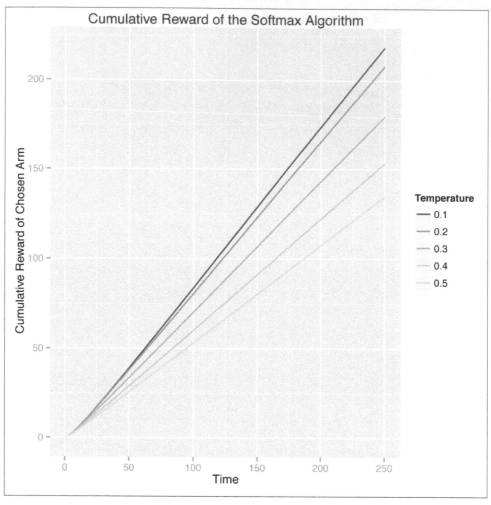

Figure 5-3. How much reward has the Softmax algorithm earned as of trial T?

The Annealing Softmax Algorithm

As we mentioned in the exercises at the end of the chapter on testing the epsilon-Greedy algorithm, it's often a good idea to encourage an algorithm to explore less over time. In the Softmax algorithm, we can achieve that by slowly decreasing the temperature, which we call *annealing*. The name annealing is based on a metaphor about blacksmithing. For a blacksmith, annealing is a process in which the blacksmith slowly decreases the temperature at which he works with molten melt so that it becomes more solid and less flexible. This is helpful for building stronger materials as the metal gets closer to its final, desired shape.

For bandit algorithms, we can metaphorically decrease the temperature by changing the temperature parameter. This will make our algorithm exploit the best arm more often and settle into its final deterministic strategy for choosing an arm. We'll set up a system to do that automatically in this last part of this chapter.

But, before we go any further, let's give two equivalent definitions of the term annealing:

- *Annealing* is the process of decreasing the temperature in a Softmax algorithm over time.

- *Annealing* is a process of modifying a bandit algorithm's behavior so that it will explore less over time.

Why are these definitions the same thing? The first definition is really a special case of the second definition, because the Softmax algorithm will explore less over time if we decrease the temperature parameter tau. So our annealing algorithm will really be a strategy for slowly lowering the temperature over time. Below, we implement a full annealing strategy, based on two simple lines of code:

```
t = sum(self.counts) + 1
temperature = 1 / math.log(t + 0.0000001)
```

What's going on here? It's easiest to understand this line by imagining what happens when t = 1. In that case, we set temperature = 1 / math.log(1.0000001), which is very close to being infinite. So the temperature is extremely high and the system will explore almost completely randomly.

But, as t goes up, the temperature will get lower and lower. Because we use logarithms, this decrease isn't extremely rapid: rather, it's just rapid enough to be effective. This division by a logarithmically scaled version of t isn't always the best approach to annealing. In the exercises for this chapter, we encourage you to play with other annealing rules that decrease the temperature faster or that decrease the temperature over discrete blocks of time, rather than on every single iteration.

Before we run those experiments, though, we need to implement the full annealing Softmax algorithm. We do that below:

```
import math
import random

def categorical_draw(probs):
  z = random.random()
  cum_prob = 0.0
  for i in range(len(probs)):
    prob = probs[i]
    cum_prob += prob
    if cum_prob > z:
      return i
```

```
      return len(probs) - 1

class AnnealingSoftmax:
  def __init__(self, counts, values):
    self.counts = counts
    self.values = values
    return

  def initialize(self, n_arms):
    self.counts = [0 for col in range(n_arms)]
    self.values = [0.0 for col in range(n_arms)]
    return

  def select_arm(self):
    t = sum(self.counts) + 1
    temperature = 1 / math.log(t + 0.0000001)

    z = sum([math.exp(v / temperature) for v in self.values])
    probs = [math.exp(v / temperature) / z for v in self.values]
    return categorical_draw(probs)

  def update(self, chosen_arm, reward):
    self.counts[chosen_arm] = self.counts[chosen_arm] + 1
    n = self.counts[chosen_arm]

    value = self.values[chosen_arm]
    new_value = ((n - 1) / float(n)) * value + (1 / float(n)) * reward
    self.values[chosen_arm] = new_value
    return
```

How useful is this change to the Softmax algorithm to make it anneal? We can judge that by running simulations of the annealing Softmax algorithm and comparing the results with our standard Softmax algorithm that used a constant temperature setting. The results are shown in Figure 5-4, Figure 5-5, and Figure 5-6.

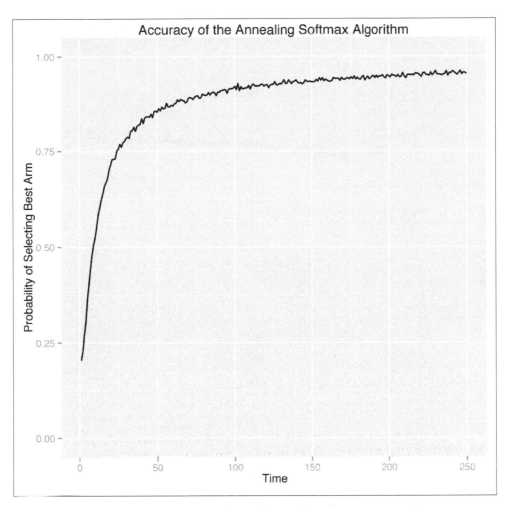

Figure 5-4. How accurate is the Annealing Softmax algorithm on average?

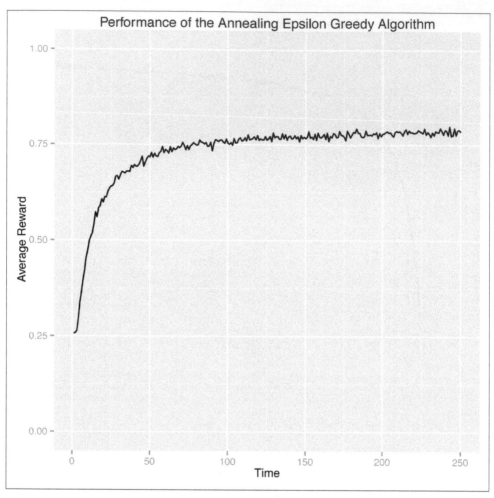

Figure 5-5. How much reward does the Annealing Softmax algorithm earn on average?

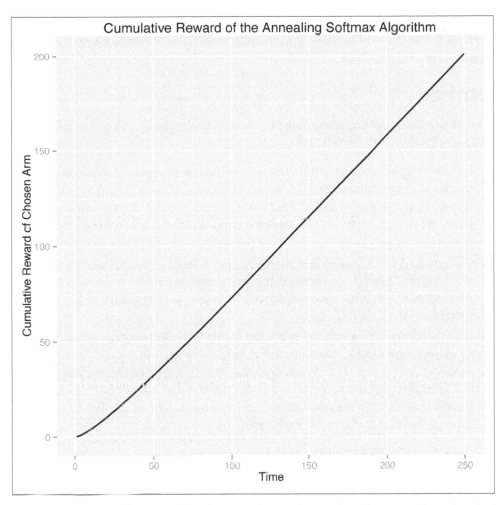

Figure 5-6. How much reward has the Annealing Softmax algorithm earned as of trial T?

As you can see by looking at these graphs, the system doesn't reach perfect performance as quickly as the best of our hard-coded temperature settings in the previous set of graphs. But the algorithm reaches its peak performance much faster than the worse of our settings and reaches a higher peaker. In many ways, it's the fact that we're doing not much worse than our best case that really matters, because we only knew which temperature setting was best *after the fact*: in practice, we'd have to experiment with different temperature settings to find one that would work well. That's a non-trivial task for a system that needs to be deployed in the real world to be fully tested, so the use of annealing can be a real improvement. You should always try to avoid being forced to use your intuition to set any parameters that can affect a bandit algorithm when it's deployed in the wild.

Of course, as always, your mileage may vary. To drive that home, we suggest some exercises below that will improve your intuitions about how softmax works and also suggest some ways in which it isn't ideal.

Exercises

In order to refine your understanding of the Softmax algorithm and its annealing variant, we suggest you try the following:

- See what happens to the Softmax algorithm if it has to explore from a set of arms that are all very similar to each and none of which stands very far out from the pack. Instead of our use of means = [0.1, 0.1, 0.1, 0.1, 0.9], try using means = [0.1, 0.1, 0.1, 0.1, 0.12]. Does the striking difference between Softmax and epsilon-Greedy go away as you change the parameters of the two algorithms?

- Can you find settings of epsilon for the epsilon-Greedy algorithm and the temperature for the Softmax algorithm that come closest to imitating one another on a fixed set of arms? What makes it difficult for these two algorithms to behave similarly?

- We used one specific annealing rule when we made the Softmax algorithm decrease its temperature setting over time. What happens when using a different rule like temperature = 1.0 / t? What happens when you change this parameter over blocks of plays so that temperature = 0.5 for the first 100 rounds and then temperature = 0.1 for the next 100 rounds? Are there general strategies for setting these parameters that seem to work well?

CHAPTER 6

UCB – The Upper Confidence Bound Algorithm

Introducing the UCB Algorithm

The algorithms we've presented so far have one systematic weakness: they don't keep track of how much they know about any of the arms available to them. They pay attention only to *how much reward they've gotten from the arms*. This means that they'll under-explore options whose initial experiences were not rewarding, even though they don't have enough data to be confident about those arms. We can do better by using an algorithm that pays attention to not only *what it knows*, but also *how much it knows*.

The algorithm, UCB, that we'll present in this chapter does exactly this. Before we describe how the UCB algorithm keeps track of how much it knows, let's look back at the epsilon-Greedy and Softmax algorithms and take a more abstract perspective on them. Both the epsilon-Greedy algorithm and the Softmax algorithm share the following broad properties:

- The algorithm's default choice is to select the arm that currently has the highest estimated value.

- The algorithm sometimes decides to explore and chooses an option that isn't the one that currently seems best:

  — The epsilon-Greedy algorithm explores by selecting from all of the arms completely at random. It makes one of these random exploratory decisions with probability `epsilon`.

— The Softmax algorithm explores by randomly selecting from all of the available arms with probabilities that are more-or-less proportional to the estimated value of each of the arms. If the other arms are noticeably worse than the best arm, they're chosen with very low probability. If the arms all have similar values, they're each chosen nearly equally often.

- In order to achieve better performance by making an effort to have these two algorithms explore less over time, both algorithms can be set up to modify their basic parameters dynamically over time. We called this modification *annealing*.

Looking at this list, we can see how UCB can improve upon the epsilon-Greedy and Softmax algorithms: it can make decisions to explore that are driven by our confidence in the estimated value of the arms we've selected.

Why is it important to keep track of our confidence in the values of the arms? The reason has to do with the nature of the rewards we receive from the arms: they're noisy. If we use our past experiences with an arm, then the estimated value of any arm is always a noisy estimate of the true return on investment we can expect from it. Because of this noise, it might just be a coincidence that Arm A seems better than Arm B; if we had more experience with both arms, we'd eventually realize that Arm B is actually better. The epsilon-Greedy and Softmax algorithms aren't robust to this noise during their first experiences with things.

Or, to put things in more human terms, the epsilon-Greedy and Softmax algorithms are *gullible*. They are easily misled by a few negative experiences. Because of their use of randomness, they can make up for this later. UCB takes a very different approach. As you'll see, UCB does not use randomness at all.

Instead, UCB avoids being gullible by requiring us to keep track of our confidence in our assessments of the estimated values of all of the arms. To do that, we need to have some metric of how much we know about each arm.

Thankfully, we already have information on hand that will give us that metric: we've been explicitly keeping track of the number of times we've pulled each arm for both of the algorithms we've used so far. Inside of the counts field in our epsilon-Greedy and Softmax classes, we have enough information to calculate a simple metric of our confidence in the estimated values of the various arms. We just need to find a way to take advantage of that information.

The UCB family of algorithms does just that. In fact, their focus on confidence is the source of the name UCB, which is an acronym for Upper Confidence Bounds. For this book, we're going to focus on only one of the algorithms in the UCB family. This special case is called the UCB1 algorithm. We'll generally refer to the UCB1 algorithm as the UCB algorithm, since it will be the only version of UCB that we'll implement.

While we won't focus on other UCB variants, we need to note that the UCB1 algorithm, unlike its siblings, makes a couple of assumptions that you may need to be cautious about. Foremost of these is the assumption that the maximum possible reward has value 1. If that's not true in your setting, you need to rescale all of your rewards to lie between 0 and 1 before using the UCB1 algorithm we present below.

In addition to explicitly keeping track of our confidence in the estimated values of each arm, the UCB algorithm is special for two other reasons:

- UCB doesn't use randomness at all. Unlike epsilon-Greedy or Softmax, it's possible to know exactly how UCB will behave in any given situation. This can make it easier to reason about at times.
- UCB doesn't have any free parameters that you need to configure before you can deploy it. This is a *major* improvement if you're interested in running it in the wild, because it means that you can start to use UCB without having a clear sense of what you expect the world to behave like.

Taken together, the use of an explicit measure of confidence, the absence of unnecessary randomness and the absence of configurable parameters makes UCB very compelling. UCB is also very easy to understand, so let's just present the algorithm and then we can continue to discuss it in more detail.

Implementing UCB

As we did with the epsilon-Greedy and Softmax algorithms, we'll start off by implementing a class to store all of the information that our algorithm needs to keep track of:

```
class UCB1():
  def __init__(self, counts, values):
    self.counts = counts
    self.values = values
    return

  def initialize(self, n_arms):
    self.counts = [0 for col in range(n_arms)]
    self.values = [0.0 for col in range(n_arms)]
    return
```

As you can see from this chunk of code, UCB doesn't have any parameters beyond the absolute minimum counts and values fields that both the epsilon-Greedy and Softmax algorithms had. The reason UCB gets away without this is how it exploits the counts field. To see UCB's for using the counts field, let's implement the select_arm and update methods:

```
def select_arm(self):
  n_arms = len(self.counts)
  for arm in range(n_arms):
    if self.counts[arm] == 0:
      return arm

  ucb_values = [0.0 for arm in range(n_arms)]
  total_counts = sum(self.counts)
  for arm in range(n_arms):
    bonus = math.sqrt((2 * math.log(total_counts)) / float(self.counts[arm]))
    ucb_values[arm] = self.values[arm] + bonus
  return ind_max(ucb_values)

def update(self, chosen_arm, reward):
  self.counts[chosen_arm] = self.counts[chosen_arm] + 1
  n = self.counts[chosen_arm]

  value = self.values[chosen_arm]
  new_value = ((n - 1) / float(n)) * value + (1 / float(n)) * reward
  self.values[chosen_arm] = new_value
  return
```

What stands out about these methods?

Let's start by focusing our attention on the `if self.counts[arm] == 0` line. What's going on here? The UCB algorithm is using this line to insure that it has played every single arm available to it at least once. This is UCB's clever trick for insuring that it doesn't have a total cold start before it starts to apply its confidence-based decision rule. It's important to keep this initialization step in mind when you consider deploying UCB1: if you will only let the algorithm run for a small number of plays (say M) and you have many arms to explore (say N), it's possible that UCB1 will just try every single arm in succession and not even make it to the end. If M < N, this is definitely going to occur. If M is close to N, you'll still spend a lot of time just doing this initial walkthrough. Whether that is a good or bad thing is something you need to consider before using UCB.

But, if you have a lot of plays ahead of you, this initial pass through all of the arms is a very good thing. It insures that the UCB algorithm knows a little bit about all available options, which makes it very effective when there are clearly inferior arms that can be essentially ignored right from start.

Once we've gotten past the initial cycling through all of the available arms, UCB1's real virtues kick in. As you can see, the `select_arm` method for UCB1 uses a special type of value that we've called a `ucb_value` in this code. The `ucb_value` combines the simple estimated value of each arm with a special bonus quantity, which is `math.sqrt((2 * math.log(total_counts)) / float(self.counts[arm]))`. The meaning of this bonus is worth pondering for a bit. The most basic statement that can be made about it is that it augments the estimated value of any arm with a measure of how much less we know about that arm than we know about the other arms. That claim can be confirmed by considering what happens if you ignore everything except for `math.log(to tal_counts) / float(self.counts[arm])`. If `counts[arm]` is small relative to `tal_counts` for a certain arm, this term will be larger than when `counts[arm]` is large relative to `total_counts`. The effect of that is that UCB is a *explicitly curious* algorithm that tries to seek out the unknown.

The other factors around this core unit of curiosity are essentially rescaling terms that make UCB work properly. For those interested in more formal details, these rescaling terms allow the algorithm to define a confidence interval that has a reasonable chance of containing the true value of the arm inside of it. UCB creates its `ucb_values` by replacing every arm's estimated value with the upper bound on the confidence interval for its value. This is why the algorithm is the *Upper Confidence Bound* algorithm.

But, setting aside issues of confidence bounds, the big idea that drives UCB is present in just dividing `math.log(total_counts))` by `float(self.counts[arm])`. As we said above, this quantity becomes a big boost in the effective value of the arm for arms that we know little about. That means that we try hard to learn about arms if we don't know enough about them, even if they seem a little worse than the best arm. In fact, this curiosity bonus means we'll even occasionally visit the worst of the arms we have available.

In fact, this curiosity bonus means that UCB can behave in very surprising ways. For example, consider the plot shown in Figure 6-1 of UCB's chances of selecting the right arm at any given point in time.

This graph looks very noisy compared with the graphs we've shown for the epsilon-Greedy and Softmax algorithm. As we noted earlier, UCB doesn't use any randomness when selecting arms. So where is the noise coming from? And why is it so striking compared with the randomized algorithms we described earlier?

The answer is surprising and reveals why the curiosity bonus that UCB has can behave in an non-intuitive way: the little dips you see in this graph come from UCB backpedaling and experimenting with inferior arms because it comes to the conclusion that it knows too little about those arms. This backpedaling matters less and less over time, but it's always present in UCB's behavior, which means that UCB doesn't become a strictly greedy algorithm even if you have a huge amount of data.

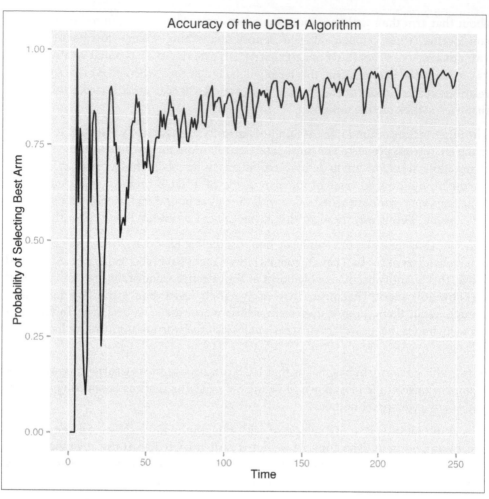

Figure 6-1. How often does the UCB1 algorithm select the best arm?

At first this backpedaling may seem troubling. To convince you that UCB is often very effective despite this counter-intuitive tendency to oscillate back into exploring inferior arms, we need to explicitly compare UCB with the other algorithms we've studied so far. This is quite easy to do, because we can simply pool all of the simulation results we've gathered so far and treat them like a single unit for analysis. In the next section, we walk through the results.

Comparing Bandit Algorithms Side-by-Side

Now that we've implemented three different algorithms for solving the Multiarmed Bandit, it's worth comparing them on a single task. As before, we've tested the algorithms using the testbed of 5 arms we've used in all of our examples so far.

For this set of comparisons, we've decided to focus on annealing versions of epsilon-Greedy and Softmax alongside UCB1. The code for both of those algorithms is available on the website for this book. Using annealing versions of the epsilon-Greedy and Softmax algorithms helps to make the comparisons with UCB1 simpler by removing parameters that have to be tuned for the epsilon-Greedy and Softmax algorithms to do their best.

In Figures Figure 6-2 through Figure 6-4, you can see the results of our three standard types of analyses for this comparison test set. In Figure 6-2, we've plotted the probability of selecting the best arm on each play by three of the algorithms we've used so far. Looking at this image, there are a few things that are striking:

- We can very clearly see how much noisier UCB1's behavior looks than the epsilon-Greedy or Softmax algorithm's.

- We see that the epsilon-Greedy algorithm doesn't converge as quickly as the Softmax algorithm. This might suggest that we need to use another annealing schedule or that this testbed is one in which the Softmax algorithm is simply superior to the epsilon-Greedy algorithm.

- We see that UCB1 takes a while to catch up with the annealing Softmax algorithm, but that it does start to catch up right near the end of the plays we've simulated. In the exercises we encourage you to try other enviroments in which UCB1 might outperform Softmax unambigiously.

- UCB1 finds the best arm very quickly, but the backpedaling it does causes it to underperform the Softmax algorithm along most metrics.

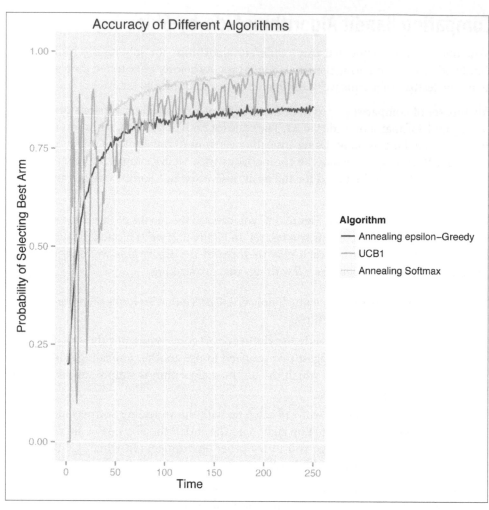

Figure 6-2. How often do our bandit algorithms select the best arm?

Looking at Figure 6-3 and Figure 6-4, we see a similar story being told by the average reward and cumulative reward.

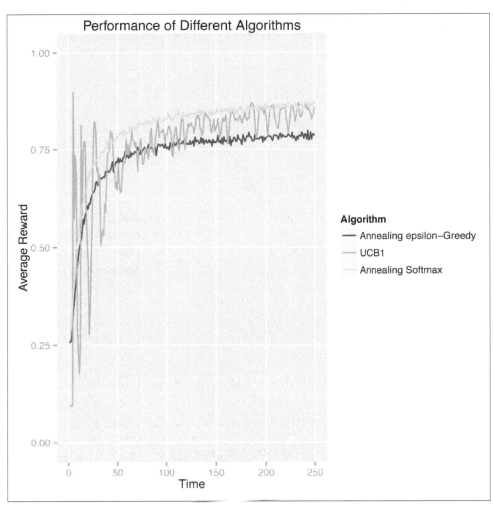

Figure 6-3. How much reward do our bandit algorithms earn on average?

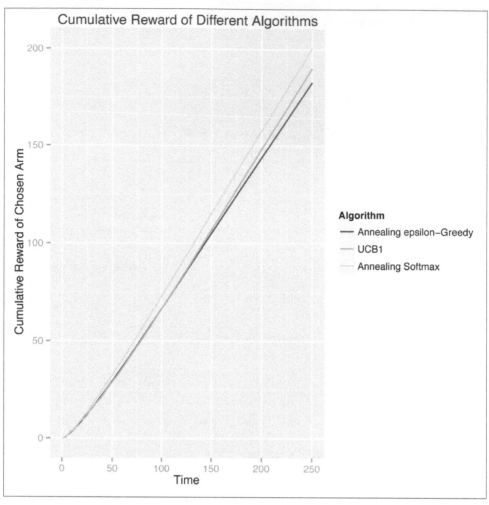

Figure 6-4. How much reward have our algorithms earned by trial T?

Exercises

UCB1 is a very powerful algorithm. In the comparisons we've just shown you, it did not outperform the epsilon-Greedy and Softmax algorithms. We'd like you to try some other simulations that will give you more insight into cases in which UCB1 will do better.

- We've already noted that the epsilon-Greedy and Softmax algorithms behave more differently in the arms in your bandit problem are very different from one another. How does the similarity between arms affect the behavior of UCB1?

- Our graphs in this chapter suggested that UCB1 would overtake the Softmax algorithm if the algorithm had run for 500 trials instead of 250. Investigate this possibility.

- Would the UCB1 algorithm perform better or worse if there were more arms? Assuming a horizon of 250 trials, how does it fare against the other algorithms when there are 20 arms? When there are 100 arms? When there are 500 arms? How does this interact with the horizon?

CHAPTER 7

Bandits in the Real World: Complexity and Complications

So far we've just given you a taste of how bandit algorithms work by showing you three standard algorithms that you can try deploying on your website. In this chapter, we want to give you some tips about ways in which the real world is likely to be more complex than the simplified examples we've used to test the algorithms we've implemented. We think that bandit algorithms are a very powerful set of tools for building better websites. But they are not a panacea. Bandit algorithms can break if the world you're exploring is more complicated than the world we've used in testing algorithms. Let's list some questions you should ask yourself when deploying bandit algorithms in the wild:

- How sure are you that you won't subtly corrupt your deployment code?
- How many different tests are you planning to run simultaneously? Will these tests interfere with each other? Will starting a new test while another one is already running corrupt its results?
- How long do you plan to run your tests?
- How many users are you willing to expose to non-preferred versions of your site?
- How well-chosen is your metric of success?
- How are the arms you're measuring related to one another?
- What additional information about context do you have when choosing arms? Do you have demographics based on browser information? Does your site have access to external information about people's tastes in products you might advertise to them?

- How much traffic does your site receive? Is the system you're building going to scale up? How much traffic can your algorithm handle before it starts to slow your site down?

- How much will you have to distort the setup we've introduced when you admit that visitors to real websites are concurrent and aren't arriving sequentially as in our simulations?

A/A Testing

Banal though it sounds, the real world is a very complicated place. The idealized scenarios we've been using in our Monte Carlo tests for evaluating the performance of different bandit algorithms are much simpler than real deployment scenarios. In the real world, both the observations you collect and the code you write to collect those observations are likely to be more complex than you realize.

The result of this complexity is that you may observe differences between two arms that are totally illusory at the same time that the data you collect will insist that those differences are significant. Researchers at Microsoft published a paper on "Trustworthy Online Controlled Experiments: Five Puzzling Outcomes Explained" that does a good job of describing some problems you are likely to run into if you deploy a bandit algorithm on your site.

One of their solutions to the problems that will come up is particularly counter-intuitive, but worth considering before we address other concerns. They want you to run A/A testing. In other words, you should use the code you develop for assigning users to arms, but then define two different arms that are actually both the same user experience. If you find differences between these two identical arms, you need to substantially temper your claims about differences between other arms. This illusory difference between two A arms may indicate that there's a bug in your code or a mistake in the way you're analyzing your data. But it may also indicate that your test is running in a context that is subtly different from the assumptions we've been implicitly making when setting up our algorithms and simulations.

Even if you try A/A testing and don't find any worring issues, this approach provides a useful way to estimate the actual variability in your data before trying to decide whether the differences found by a bandit algorithm are real. And that matters a lot if your plan is to use a bandit algorithm not as a permanent feature of your site, but as a one-off experiment.

Running Concurrent Experiments

While we've discussed algorithms that can cope with a few arms that are well-separated, many real-world websites will end up running many different experiments simultaneously. These experiments will end up overlapping: a site may use A/B testing to compare two different logo colors while also using A/B testing to compare two different fonts. Even the existence of one extra test that's not relating to the arms you're comparing can add a lot of uncertainty into your results. Things may still work out well. But your experiments may also turn out very badly if the concurrent changes you're making to your site don't play well together and have strange interactions.

In an ideal world, concurrency issues raised by running multiple experiments at once won't come up. You'll be aware that you have lots of different questions and so you would plan all of your tests in one giant group. Then you would define your arms in terms of the combinations of all the factors you want to test: if you were testing both colors and fonts, you'd have one arm for every color/font pair.

This ideal world fails not only because people get sparks of inspiration that make them change course over time. It also fails because the number of arms you would need to test can quickly blow up if you start combining the different factors you want to test into separate pairs. Of course, if you don't keep track of other tests, you may end up with a large number of puzzling results that are all artifacts of running so many experiments simultaneously.

The best solution to this is simple: *try your best to keep track of all of the experiments each user is a part of and include this information in your analyses of any single experiment.*

Continuous Experimentation vs. Periodic Testing

Are you planning to run tests for a while to decide which approaches are best? Are you then going to stop running new experiments after you've made that decision? In that case, A/B testing may often be wise if you have a similar set of proposed changes that would become arms in your Multiarmed Bandit setup. If you're doing short-term experiments, it's often not so important to avoid testing inferior strategies because the consequences aren't so bad.

But if you're willing to let your experiments run much longer, turning things over to a bandit algorithm can be a huge gain because the algorithm will automatically start to filter out inferior designs over time without requiring you to make a judgment call. Whether this is a good thing or not really depends on the details of your situation. But the general point stands: *bandit algorithms look much better than A/B testing when you are willing to let them run for a very long time.* If you're willing to have your site perpetually be in a state of experimentation, bandit algorithms will be *many times better* than A/B testing.

A related issue to the contrast between continuous experimentation versus short periods of experimentation is the question of how many users should be in your experiments. You'll get the most data if you put more users into your test group, but you risk alienating more of them if you test something that's really unpopular. The answers to this question don't depend on whether you're using bandit algorithm or A/B testing, but the answers will affect how well a bandit algorithm can work in your setting. If you run a bandit algorithm on a very small number of users, you may end up with too little data about the arms that the algorithm decided were inferior to make very strong conclusions about them in the future. A/B testing's preference for balancing people across arms can be advantageous if you aren't going to gather a lot of data.

Bad Metrics of Success

The core premise of using a bandit algorithm is that you have a well-defined measure of reward that you want to maximize. A real business is much more complicated than this simple setup might suggest. One potentially fatal source of increased complexity is that optimizing short-term click-through rates may destroy the long-term retainability of your users. Greg Linden, one of the earlier developers of A/B testing tools at Amazon, says that this kind of thing actually happened to Amazon in the 1990's when they first started doing automatic A/B testing. The tools that were ostensibly optimizing their chosen metric were actually harming Amazon's long-term business. Amazon was able to resolve the situation, but the problem of optimizing the wrong metric of success is so ubiquitous that it's likely other businesses have lost a great deal more than Amazon did because of poorly chosen metrics.

Unfortunately, there's no algorithmic solution to this problem. Once you decide to start working with automated metrics, you need to supplement those systems by exercising human judgment and making sure that you keep an eye on what happens as the system makes changes to your site.

Monitoring many different metrics you think are important to your business is probably the best thing you can hope do. For example, creating an aggregate site well-being score that simply averages together a lot of different metrics you want to optimize may often be a better measure of success than any single metric you would try in isolation.

Scaling Problems with Good Metrics of Success

Even if you have a good metric of success, like the total amount of purchases made by a client over a period of a year, the algorithms described in this book may not work well unless you rescale those metrics into the 0-1 space we've used in our examples. The reasons for this are quite boring: some of the algorithms are numerically unstable, especially the softmax algorithm, which will break down if you start trying to calculate things like $\exp(10000.0)$. You need to make sure that you've scaled the rewards in your problem into a range in which the algorithms will be numerically stable. If you can, try to use the 0-1 scale we've used, which is, as we briefly noted earlier, an absolute requirement if you plan on using the UCB1 algorithm.

Intelligent Initialization of Values

In the section on the epsilon-Greedy algorithm, we mentioned how important it is to consider how you initialize the values of arms you've never explored. In the real world, you can often do this using information you have before ever deploying a bandit algorithm. This smart initialization can happen in two ways.

First, you can use the historical metrics for the control arm in your bandit algorithm. Whatever arm corresponds to how your site traditionally behaved can be given an initial value based on data from before you let the bandit algorithm loose. In addition, you can initialize all of the unfamiliar arms using this same approach.

Second, you can use the amount of historical data you have to calibrate how much the algorithm thinks you know about the historical options. For an algorithm like UCB1, that will strongly encourage the algorithm to explore new options until the algorithm has some confidence about their worth relative to tradition. This can be a very good thing, although it needs to be done with caution.

Running Better Simulations

In addition to initializing your algorithm using prior information you have before deploying a Bandit algorithm, you can often run much better simulations if you use historical information to build appropriate simulations. In this book we've used a toy Monte Carlo simulation with click-through rates that varied from 0.1 to 0.9. Real world click-through rates are typically much lower than this. Because low success rates may mean that your algorithm must run for a very long time before it is able to reach any strong conclusions, you should conduct simulations that are informed by real data about your business if you have access to it.

Moving Worlds

In the real world, the value of different arms in a bandit problem can easily change over time. As we said in the introduction, an orange and black site design might be perfect during Halloween, but terrible during Christmas. Because the true value of an arm might actually shift over time, you want your estimates to be able to do this as well.

Arms with changing values can be a very serious problem if you're not careful when you deploy a bandit algorithm. The algorithms we've presented will not handle most sorts of change in the underlying values of arms well. The problem has to do with the way that we estimate the value of an arm. We typically updated our estimates using the following snippet of code:

```
new_value = ((n - 1) / float(n)) * value + (1 / float(n)) * reward
self.values[chosen_arm] = new_value
```

The problem with this update rule is that `1 / float(n)` goes to 0 as n gets large. When you're dealing with millions or billions of plays, this means that recent rewards will have almost zero effect on your estimates of the value of different arms. If those values shifted only a small amount, the algorithm will take a huge number of plays to update its estimated values.

There is a simple trick for working around this that can be used if you're careful: instead of estimating the values of the arms using strict averages, you can overweight recent events by using a slightly different update rule based on a different snippet of code:

```
new_value = (1 - alpha) * value + (alpha) * reward
self.values[chosen_arm] = new_value
```

In the traditional rule, `alpha` changed from trial to trial. In this alternative, `alpha` is a fixed value between `0.0` and `1.0`. This alternative updating rule will allow your estimates to shift much more with recent experiences. When the world can change radically, that flexibility is very important.

Unfortunately, the price you pay for that flexibility is the introduction of a new parameter that you'll have to tune to your specific business. We encourage you to experiment with this modified updating rule using simulations to develop an intuition for how it behaves in environments like yours. If used appropriately in a changing world, setting `alpha` to a constant value can make a big difference relative to allowing `alpha` to go to `0` too quickly. But, if used carelessly, this same change will make your algorithm behave erratically. If you set `alpha = 1.0`, you can expect to unleash a nightmare for yourself.

Correlated Bandits

In many situations, you want to solve a Multiarmed Bandit Problem with a large number of arms. This will be hopeless unless there is some way you can generalize your experiences with some arms to other arms. When you can make generalizations safely, we say that the arms are correlated. To be extremely precise, what matters is that the expected rewards of different arms are correlated.

To illustrate this idea, let's go back to our earlier idea about experimenting with different color logos. It's reasonable to assume that similar colors are likely to elicit similar reactions. So you might try to propagate information about rewards from one color to other colors based on their degree of similarity.

If you're working with thousands of colors, simple algorithms like UCB1 may not be appropriate because they can't exploit the correlations across colors. You'll need to find ways to relate arms and update your estimates based on this information. In this short book we don't have time to get into issues much, but we encourage you to look into classical smoothing techniques in statistics to get a sense for how you might deal with correlated arms.

Contextual Bandits

In addition to correlations between arms in a bandit task, it's often the case that we have background information about the context in which we're trying out different options. For example, we may find that certain fonts are more appealing to male users than to female users. We refer to this side information as context. There are a variety of algorithms like LinUCB and GLMUCB for working with contextual information: you can read about them in two academic papers called "A Contextual-Bandit Approach to Personalized News Article Recommendation" and "Parametric Bandits: The Generalized Linear Case".

Both of these algorithms are more complicated than the algorithms we've covered in this book, but the spirit of these models is easy to describe: you want to develop a predictive model of the value of arms that depends upon context. You can use any of the techniques available in conventional machine learning for doing this. If those techniques allow you to update your model using online learning, you can build a contextual bandit algorithm out of them.

LinUCB does this by updating a linear regression model for the arms' values after each play. GLMUCB does this by updating a General Linear Model for the arms' values after each play. Many other algorithms exist and you could create your own with some research into online versions of your favorite machine learning algorithm.

Implementing Bandit Algorithms at Scale

Many of the topics we've discussed make bandit algorithms more complex in order to cope with the complexity of the real world. But that complexity may make deploying a bandit algorithm prohibitively difficult at scale. Why is that?

Even in the simplest real-world settings, the bandit algorithms we've described in this book may not work as well as they do in simulations because you often may not know what happened on your N-th play in the real world until a while after you've been forced to serve a new page for (and therefore select a new arm for) many other users. This destroys the clean sequential structure we've assumed throughout the book. If you're a website that serves hundreds of thousands of hits in a second, this can be a very substantial break from the scenarios we've been envisoning.

This is only one example of how the algorithms we've described are non-trivial when you want to get them to scale up, but we'll focus on it for the sake of brevity. Our proposed solution seems to be the solution chosen by Google for Google Analytics based on information in their help documents, although we don't know the details of how their system is configured.

In short, our approach to dealing with imperfect sequential assignments is to embrace this failure and develop a system that is easier to scale up. We propose doing this in two parts:

Blocked assignments
> Assign incoming users to new arms in advance and draw this information from a fast cache when users actually arrive. Store their responses for batch processing later in another fast cache.

Blocked updates
> Update your estimates of arm values in batches on a regular interval and regenerate your blocked assignments. Because you work in batches, it will be easier to perform the kind of complex calculations you'll need to deal with correlated arms or contextual information.

Changes like this can go a long way in making bandit algorithms scale up for large websites. But, once you start to make changes to bandit algorithms to deal with these sorts of scale problems, you'll find that the theoretical literature on bandits often becomes less informative about what you can expect will happen. There are a few papers that have recently come out: if you're interested, this problem is referred to as the problem of *delayed feedback* in the academic literature.

Thankfully, even though the academic literature is a little sparser on the topic of delayed feedback, you can still run Monte Carlo simulations to test your approach before deploying a bandit system that has to cope with delayed feedback. Of course, you'll have to make simulations that are more complex than those we've described already, but those more complex simulations are still possible to design. And they may convince you that your proposed algorithms works even though you're working in uncharted waters beyond what theoreticians have studied. That's the reason we've focused on using simulations through the book. We want you to feel comfortable exploring this topic for yourself, even when doing so will take you into areas that science hasn't fully reached yet.

While you're exploring, you'll come up with lots of other interesting questions about scaling up bandit algorithms like:

- What sort of database should you store information in? Is something like MySQL usable or do you need to work with something like Memcached? If you need to pull out assignments to arms quickly, it's probably wise to move this information into the lowest latency data storage tool you have available to you.

- Where in your production code should you be running the equivalent of our `select_arm` and `update` functions? In the blocked assignments model we described earlier, this happens far removed from the tools that directly generate served pages. But in the obvious strategy for deploying bandit algorithms, this happens in the page generation mechanism itself.

We hope you enjoy the challenges that making bandit algorithms work in large production environments can pose. We think this is one of the most interesting questions in engineering today.

CHAPTER 8

Conclusion

Learning Life Lessons from Bandit Algorithms

In this book, we've presented three algorithms for solving the Multiarmed Bandit Problem:

- The epsilon-Greedy Algorithm
- The Softmax Algorithm
- The UCB Algorithm

In order to really take advantage of these three algorithms, you'll need to develop a good intuition for how they'll behave when you deploy them on a live website. Having an intuition about which algorithms will work in practice is important because there is no universal bandit algorithm that will always do the best job of optimizing a website: domain expertise and good judgment will always be necessary.

To help you develop the intuition and judgment you'll need, we've advocated a Monte Carlo simulation framework that lets you see how these algorithms and others will behave in hypothetical worlds. By testing an algorithm in many different hypothetical worlds, you can build an appreciation for the qualitative dynamics that cause a bandit algorithm to succeed in one scenario and to fail in another.

In this last section, we'd like to help you further down that path by highlighting these qualitative patterns explicitly.

We'll start off with some general life lessons that we think are exemplified by bandit algorithms, but actually apply to any situation you might ever find yourself in. Here are the most salient lessons:

Trade-offs, trade-offs, trade-offs

In the real world, you *always* have to trade off between gathering data and acting on that data. Pure experimentation in the form of exploration is always a short-term loss, but pure profit-making in the form of exploitation is always blind to the long-term benefits of curiosity and openmindedness. You can be clever about the compromises you make, but you will have to make some compromises.

God does play dice

Randomization is the key to the good life. Controlled experiments online won't work without randomization. If you want to learn from your experiences, you need to be in complete control of those experiences. While the UCB algorithms we've used in this book aren't truly randomized, they behave at least partially like randomized algorithms from the perspective of your users. Ultimately what matters most is that you make sure that end-users can't self-select into the arms you want to experiment with.

Defaults matter a lot

The way in which you initialize an algorithm can have a powerful effect on its long-term success. You need to figure out whether your biases are helping you or hurting you. No matter what you do, you will be biased in some way or another. What matters is that you spend some time learning whether your biases help or hurt. Part of the genius of the UCB family of algorithms is that they make a point to do this initialization in a very systematic way right at the start.

Take a chance

You should try everything at the start of your explorations to insure that you know a little bit about the potential value of every option. Don't close your mind without giving something a fair shot. At the same time, just one experience should be enough to convince you that some mistakes aren't worth repeating.

Everybody's gotta grow up sometime

You should make sure that you explore less over time. No matter what you're doing, it's important that you don't spend your whole life trying out every crazy idea that comes into your head. In the bandit algorithms we've tried, we've seen this lesson play out when we've implemented annealing. The UCB algorithms achieve similar effects to annealing by explicitly counting their experiences with different arms. Either strategy is better than not taking any steps to become more conservative over time.

Leave your mistakes behind

You should direct your exploration to focus on the second-best option, the third-best option and a few other options that are just a little bit further away from the best. Don't waste much or any of your time on options that are clearly losing bets. Naive experimentation of the sort that occurs in A/B testing is often a deadweight loss if some of the ideas you're experimenting with are disasters waiting to happen.

Don't be cocky

You should keep track of how confident you are about your evaluations of each of the options available to you. Don't be close-minded when you don't have evidence to support your beliefs. At the same time, don't be so unsure of yourself that you forget how much you already know. Measuring one's confidence explicitly is what makes UCB so much more effective than either the epsilon-Greedy algorithm or the Softmax algorithm in some settings.

Context matters

You should use any and every piece of information you have available to you about the context of your experiments. Don't simplify the world too much and pretend you've got things figured out: there's more to optimizing your business that comparing A with B. If you can figure out a way to exploit context using strategies like those seen in the contextual bandit algorithms we briefly discussed, use them. And if there are ways to generalize your experiences across arms, take advantage of them.

A Taxonomy of Bandit Algorithms

To help your remember how these lessons relate to the algorithms we've described, here are six dimensions along which you can measure most bandit algorithms you'll come across, including all of the algorithms presented in this book: .

1. *Curiosity*: Does the algorithm keep track of how much it knows about each arm? Does the algorithm try to gain knowledge explicitly, rather than incidentally? In other words, is the algorithm curious?

2. *Increased Exploitation over Time*: Does the algorithm explicitly try to explore less over time? In other words, does the algorithm use annealing?

3. *Strategic Exploration*: What factors determine the algorithm's decision at each time point? Does it maximize reward, knowledge, or a combination of the two?

4. *Number of Tunable Parameters*: How many parameters does the algorithm have? Since you have to tune these parameters, it's generally better to use algorithms that have fewer parameters.

5. *Initialization Strategy*: What assumptions does the algorithm make about the value of arms it has not yet explored?

6. *Context-Aware*: Is the algorithm able to use background context about the value of the arms?

Learning More and Other Topics

Hopefully this book has gotten you interested in bandit algorithms. While you could easily spend the rest your life tinkering with the simulation framework we've given you to find the best possible settings of different parameters for the algorithms we've described, it's probably better for you to read about how other people are using bandit algorithms. Here's a very partial reading list we'd suggest for those interested:

- If you're interested in digging into the academic literature on the Multiarmed Bandit Problem, the best introduction is probably in the classic textbook on Reinforcement Learning, which is a broader topic than the Multiarmed Bandit Problem:

  — *Reinforcement Learning: An Introduction* by Richard S. Sutton and Andrew G. Barto, (1998).

- A good starting point for going beyond Sutton and Barto's introduction is to read about some of the other bandit algorithms out there that we didn't have time to discuss in this book. As time goes on, we will implement more of those algorithms and place them on the website for this book. In addition to exploring the supplemental code that is already available on the website, you might be interested in going to the primary sources and reading about the following other algorithms for dealing with the Multiarmed Bandit Problem:

  — *Exp3*: You can read about Exp3 in "The Nonstochastic Multiarmed Bandit Problem" by Auer et al., (2001).

  — *Exp4*: You can also read about Exp4 in "The Nonstochastic Multiarmed Bandit Problem" by Auer et al. (2001).

  — *The Knowledge Gradient*: You can read about the Knowledge Gradient in "A knowledge-gradient policy for sequential information collection" by Frazier et al. (2008).

  — *Randomized Probability Matching*: You can read about Randomized Probability Matching in "A modern Bayesian look at the multiarmed bandit" by Steven L. Scott. (2010).

  — *Thompson Sampling*: You can read about Thompson Sampling in "An Empirical Evaluation of Thompson Sampling" by Olivier Chapelle and Lihong Li. (2011).

- If you're interested in contextual bandit algorithms like LinUCB and GLMUCB, you might look at:

  — *LinUCB*: "A Contextual-Bandit Approach to Personalized News Article Recommendation" by Li et al. (2010).

  — *GLMUCB*: "Parametric Bandits: The Generalized Linear Case" by Filippi et al. (2010).

- If you're ready to do some much heavier reading on this subject, you might benefit from some of the best recent review papers discussing bandit algorithms:
  - "Sequential Decision Making in Non-stochastic Environments" by Jacob Abernethy (2012).
  - "Online Learning and Online Convex Optimization" by Shai Shalev-Shwartz (2012).
- If you're interested in reading about how Yahoo! used bandit algorithms in its business, John Langford and colleagues have written many interesting papers and presentations including:
  - "Learning for Contextual Bandits" by Alina Beygelzimer and John Langford (2011).
  - "Contextual-Bandit Approach to Personalized News Article Recommendation" by Lihong Li et al. (2010).

About the Author

John Myles White is a Ph.D. student in the Princeton Psychology Department, where he studies behavioral decision theory. Along with Drew Conway, he is the author of the book *Machine Learning for Hackers* (O'Reilly). John has worked on several popular R packages, including ProjectTemplate and log4r, and is currently working on building statistical packages for the new programming language Julia.

Colophon

The animal on the cover of *Bandit Algorithms for Website Optimization* is the eastern barred bandicoot (*Perameles gunnii*). There are two subspecies, both of which inhabit southeastern Australia. The subspecies that lives in Victoria is considered critically endangered despite restoration efforts by conservationists. The other subspecies lives in Tasmania. Barred banidcoots will typically make and live in ground nests made up of grass, leaves, and twigs.

The eastern barred bandicoot is a small marsupial that weighs around 2 pounds. This species of bandicoot is distinctive for its three to four bars on its hindquarters. It is nocturnal, feeding at night on insects and plants. With its claws and long snout, it will dig holes in the ground to find its food. The typical life span of the eastern barred bandicoot is two to three years.

The cover image is from Wood's *Animate Creations*. The cover font is Adobe ITC Garamond. The text font is Adobe Minion Pro; the heading font is Adobe Myriad Condensed; and the code font is Dalton Maag's Ubuntu Mono.

Have it your way.

O'Reilly eBooks

- Lifetime access to the book when you buy through oreilly.com

- Provided in up to four DRM-free file formats, for use on the devices of your choice: PDF, .epub, Kindle-compatible .mobi, and Android .apk

- Fully searchable, with copy-and-paste and print functionality

- Alerts when files are updated with corrections and additions

oreilly.com/ebooks/

Safari Books Online

- Access the contents and quickly search over 7000 books on technology, business, and certification guides

- Learn from expert video tutorials, and explore thousands of hours of video on technology and design topics

- Download whole books or chapters in PDF format, at no extra cost, to print or read on the go

- Get early access to books as they're being written

- Interact directly with authors of upcoming books

- Save up to 35% on O'Reilly print books

See the complete Safari Library at safari.oreilly.com

O'REILLY®

Get even more for your money.

Join the O'Reilly Community, and register the O'Reilly books you own. It's free, and you'll get:

- $4.99 ebook upgrade offer
- 40% upgrade offer on O'Reilly print books
- Membership discounts on books and events
- Free lifetime updates to ebooks and videos
- Multiple ebook formats, DRM FREE
- Participation in the O'Reilly community
- Newsletters
- Account management
- 100% Satisfaction Guarantee

Signing up is easy:

1. **Go to: oreilly.com/go/register**
2. **Create an O'Reilly login.**
3. **Provide your address.**
4. **Register your books.**

Note: English-language books only

To order books online:
oreilly.com/store

For questions about products or an order:
orders@oreilly.com

To sign up to get topic-specific email announcements and/or news about upcoming books, conferences, special offers, and new technologies:
elists@oreilly.com

For technical questions about book content:
booktech@oreilly.com

To submit new book proposals to our editors:
proposals@oreilly.com

O'Reilly books are available in multiple DRM-free ebook formats. For more information:
oreilly.com/ebooks

O'REILLY®

Spreading the knowledge of innovators   oreilly.com

9 781449 341336